PARIS

Barbara Ender and Ken Bernstein

J·P·M
PUBLICATIONS

CONTENTS

This Way Paris

You'll Be Back

There must be something infectious in the air of Paris, making you want to go back time and again. The addiction strikes as soon as you arrive. Certainly the first visit is no more than an appetizer, as unassuming as a slice of pâté and a pickle on the kind of bread that no one could imitate at home. You may have seen the new Louvre—well, the *Mona Lisa* and an hour of trudging—and looked down on the city from the Eiffel Tower and gazed up at it from a sightseeing boat on the Seine, but so much has still to be accomplished. You've hardly spoken to a genuine Parisian, or figured out what makes them so damn *chic*. You've barely attempted the bright, efficient transit system and there hasn't been much time or energy to walk along the river or under the giant chestnut trees, in what is the world's most walkable capital. You can't quite remember whether you're on the Right Bank or the Left, or what the difference means. The itch has already begun; a return trip to Paris is definitely due. Almost before you've got to grips with the first one.

Up the Cathedral

If you're not on the Right Bank nor the Left, chances are you're on the streamlined island in the middle of the Seine, the Ile de la Cité. And the wonderful medieval cathedral you're looking at is Notre-Dame de Paris. You could spend an hour in the plaza out front just marvelling at the harmony and the sculptural details. But go inside and up top for one of the city's greatest panoramas.

Heaven knows, Paris has enough superb historic churches to keep a pilgrim busy round the clock. But nearby you'll always find a café to catch your breath, and a restaurant to revive your faith in the creativity of France's farmers and cooks.

The New Paris

Even if you had seen all the historic monuments you'd have to come back to catch up with the breathtaking changes in Paris. Just the past few years have added revolutionary new attractions, starting with I.M. Pei's glass pyramid smack in the middle of the new, enlarged, improved Louvre. Another kind of magic turned an old railway station into the Musée d'Orsay,

Place de la Concorde, with, for once, the waterworks switched off.

as exciting as a museum can be. Spectacular in a bigger way is the Arche de la Défense, a hollow marble cube 110 m (360 ft) high that opens new perspectives of architecture and city planning. Then there is the ambitious but not pompous City of Music; and the final controversial monument to the intellectual era of François Mitterrand, the (Very) Great Library. Nobody has ever skimped on culture in Paris, the City of Light.

It's Always Sunny

Somehow the imagination always paints a Paris as sunny as a lazy summer picnic. In truth, in winter Paris can be even rainier than London. So say the statistics—but what do the weathermen know about romance? If you're waiting out a squall in a welcoming bistro, a department store crammed with flair, or a musty bookshop, you're keeping dry but drenched in the spirit of Paris. And, when it's over, even the puddles reflect the grace of the city—the wrought-iron railings, the shop-fronts, the sculpture. Water is an essential part of Paris, from the fountains and the ponds for mini-sailboats to the irresistible tide of the Seine, to the early morning ceremony of the washing of the streets.

Flashback

In Roman Times

The history of Paris goes back a couple of thousand years to the time of Julius Caesar. The original fishermen's town, on the Ile de la Cité, didn't amount to much. The Right Bank was too marshy, so Paris expanded to what is now, by almost total coincidence, called the Latin Quarter. A 6th-century bishop of Paris, St Germain, was buried in an abbey out in a Left Bank suburb, now the city's oldest church, St Germain des Prés. Until the 10th century, the city remained, for practical and political purposes, as provincial as a fish market.

Capital City

In AD 987 the nobles and clergy elected Hugues Capet, Count of Paris, the King of France. With Paris as his capital, he founded a dynasty that endured for centuries. His successors expanded the city and its power, and by the 12th century Paris had taken on its present social pattern: political authority on the island, culture on the Left Bank, business on the Right Bank. In 1215, Pope Innocent III granted a charter to the University of Paris; the Latin Quarter was so called because the thousands of students there were taught in Latin. During this time the first Louvre fortress and the Gothic Cathedral of Notre-Dame were begun.

English Paris

Here's an ironic twist: at the beginning of the 15th century the English captured Paris. Joan of Arc tried to toss them out, but in vain. In 1431, England's very young King Henry VI was crowned King of France in Notre-Dame. He didn't last long—barely five years—but it was more than a grim little footnote for the patriotic French. There followed a plague that wiped out thousands.

French Grandeur

Palaces and mansions proliferated in Paris as the Renaissance arrived in the 16th century. The Louvre, originally a utilitarian fortress, evolved into a palace and an ornate Hotel de Ville took over as the headquarters of municipal power. By the beginning of the 17th century Paris was Europe's biggest city and most brilliant capital.

But troubles and mass murder spoiled the charm. Catholic Paris turned on its Protestants in 1572, and in the St Bartholomew's Eve Massacre thousands of Huguenots were slain. Religious wars and skirmishes continued until 1598 and the Edict of Nantes.

The arrogant Louis XIV may have turned his back on Paris, moving his court to the suburban opulence of Versailles, but it was nonetheless a good era for the capital city. Thank Louis for planning the massive veterans' hospital, Les Invalides, and the landscaped delights of the Tuileries and the Champs-Elysées. On a more practical note, the Sun King also illuminated Paris with street lighting.

Revolution

On July 14, 1789, hungry and abused, the people of Paris rose up against their rulers, storming the prison-fortress of the Bastille. The king and queen were beheaded. Two centuries later, in 1989, demonstrations on the Place de la Concorde during the celebration of the Bicentenary of the Revolution commemorated good old King Louis, on the very spot where he had lost his head. Today's Parisians, Republicans at heart, prefer to remember the Declaration of the Rights of Man, rather than the terrors.

Under Napoleon Bonaparte, the capital gained grandiose landmarks like the Arc de Triomphe and the star-burst of avenues spreading out from the Etoile, but he also contributed practical innovations like food markets and waterworks. In size and power, Paris was on the upswing. Bonaparte's nephew, Napoleon III, assigned the formidable city planner, Baron Haussmann, to visionary feats of urbanization. Down came overcrowded, depressed housing districts, replaced by wide, tree-lined boulevards and parks, and the new Opéra. The working classes displaced by this scheme started heading outwards to the new suburbs.

Artists and Writers

By the beginning of the 20th century Paris was so incomparably beautiful and inspiring that artists and writers moved in from all over the world. Ocean liners disgorged the Hemingways and Fitzgeralds, plus many more who had to try the "Paris experience" to realize that they would never win fame and glory. Artists from all over Europe and beyond discovered cubism and surrealism, and the famous cafés of St Germain des Prés, the Flore, the Deux Magots, provided refuge for poets, writers and philosophers inventing existentialism or non-starter "isms".

La Villette: the old abattoir district transformed into a vibrant, cultural complex, all set for the 21st century.

In the cellars of Paris, *le jazz hot* took on a new life. It may apply universally, but *avant-garde* is a distinctly French expression.

After the War

Because of the German occupation of Paris, World War II left deep, often secret scars in the hearts of Frenchmen. In May 1968, while American youngsters were protesting against the Vietnam War, Paris students violently took to the streets in frustration at the Fifth Republic of General de Gaulle. Street battles and barricades led to general strikes, paralyzing the whole country. De Gaulle retired after defeat in a referendum held in 1969.

Subsequent presidents dedicated themselves to leaving cultural monuments for the ages, from the eternally controversial but wildly popular Pompidou Centre to the much-disparaged Bastille Opera, the gleaming white building that everyone loves to hate. Even the world's most famous strolling street, the Champs-Elysées, is looking better than ever.

You may have to restrain your nostalgia to live hand in hand with change, but you're bound to conclude that Paris has never been more magnificent.

Landmarks

Our "monumental" tour of Paris begins at its very heart, on the Ile de la Cité, and follows the spiral of its 20 arrondissements (districts) as far as the Grande Arche de la Défense, on the threshold of the 21st century. The crowd-pullers are Notre-Dame, the Eiffel Tower, Sacré-Cœur and the Arc de Triomphe.

NOTRE-DAME DE PARIS

Ⓜ *Cité*
Place du Parvis Notre-Dame (4th)
Open daily 8 a.m.–7 p.m. (closed Saturday noon–2 p.m.)
Treasury open 9.30 a.m.–5 p.m. (closed Sunday).

Begun in 1163 by Bishop Maurice de Sully, the Gothic cathedral was completed more than 180 years later and then restored by Viollet-le-Duc from 1845 to 1864. Stretching across the entire width of the façade, over the three main doorways, the restored Gallery of Kings consists of 28 statues representing the kings of Judah and Israel. These were pulled down during the Revolution as they were thought to be the kings of France.

The original heads, rather battered, are on view in the Musée de Cluny. Inside the cathedral, admire the two huge rose windows: the 13th-century blue north window illustrates the Old Testament, whereas scenes from the New Testament are portrayed in the red south window.

The door to the towers is outside, on the north side. Tackle the 387 winding stairs for a close-up view of the stone monsters which have watched over the city for centuries.

PALAIS DE JUSTICE

Ⓜ *Cité*
2, bd du Palais (1st)
Open daily 9 a.m.–5 p.m.

Before they moved to the Louvre, the French kings ruled from the buildings that cover the western end of the Ile de la Cité, today comprising the Palais de Justice (Law Courts), the Conciergerie and the Sainte-Chapelle. Once past the security check you can mingle with barristers, witnesses, plaintiffs and reporters biding time in the Salle des Pas Perdus. If you want to watch French law in action, attend one of the public sessions held from 1.30 p.m.

CONCIERGERIE

Ⓜ *Cité or* Ⓡ *Saint-Michel*
1, quai de l'Horloge (1st)
Open daily 9.30 a.m.–6.30 p.m. (winter 10 a.m.–5 p.m.). Closed on public holidays.

With slate-blue roofs and pepperpot towers, this building originally included the living quarters of the concierge in charge of the criminals locked up there. During the Revolution, Marie-Antoinette, Robespierre and Danton spent their last days in its dank cells, waiting to be carted off to the guillotine.

SAINTE-CHAPELLE

Ⓜ *Cité or* Ⓡ *Saint-Michel*
4, bd du Palais (1st)
Open daily 10 a.m.–5 p.m.

This 13th-century chapel was built by Louis IX (Saint Louis) to house the Crown of Thorns and a fragment of the True Cross that he had obtained from the emperor of Constantinople. The 15 tall stained-glass windows form a dazzling wall of colour.

ÉGLISE SAINT-EUSTACHE

Ⓜ *Les Halles*
2, rue du Jour (1st)

The Parisians didn't see this beautiful Flamboyant Gothic church properly until the old central market of Les Halles was demolished. Both Liszt and Berlioz gave organ recitals here. The stained-glass windows, dating from the 17th century, were crafted according to medieval traditions.

HÔTEL DE VILLE
Ⓜ *Hôtel de Ville*
Place de l'Hôtel de Ville (4th)
The Town Hall was rebuilt in
neo-Renaissance style just three
years after supporters of the
Commune sent the old one up in
flames. The façade's 136 statues
represent French citizens (the males)
and French towns (the females).

ARÈNES DE LUTÈCE
Ⓜ *Cardinal Lemoine*
47, rue Monge (5th)
Open daily 8 a.m.–10 p.m.
(winter 8 a.m.–5.30 p.m.).
The ancient amphitheatre is the only
Parisian monument remaining from
Gallo-Roman times, apart from the
Baths of Cluny.

MOSQUÉE
Ⓜ *Place Monge*
Place du Puits-de-l'Ermite (5th)
Off the beaten Latin Quarter track,
this mosque was built in the 1920s
in Moorish style with marble
colonnade and mosaic friezes.
Sample mint tea and Arab pastries
in the tea-room. The entrance to the
hammam (steam baths) is at 39, rue
Geoffrey-Saint-Hilaire.

PANTHÉON
Ⓜ *Cardinal Lemoine or*
ⓇⒺⓇ *Luxembourg*
Place du Panthéon (5th)
Open daily 9.30 a.m.–6.30 p.m.
(winter 10 a.m.–5.30 p.m.) Closed
on public holidays.
This last resting place of France's
great men—among them Voltaire,
Rousseau, Victor Hugo, Jean Moulin,
Jean Monnet and André Malraux—
was originally designed by Soufflot
as a church for Louis XV. During the
Revolution it was secularized as a
mausoleum, Napoleon turned it back
into a church and it shifted between
secular and consecrated status until
Victor Hugo's funeral in 1885. Only
the dome, the nave and the crypt are
open to the public.

SORBONNE
ⓇⒺⓇ *Luxembourg*
Place de la Sorbonne (5th)
Robert de Sorbon, the chaplain of
Louis IX, founded the university in
1257 as a college for impoverished
theological students. Richelieu, who
financed reconstruction in 1642, is
buried in the chapel (closed to the
public). You can see the grand
amphitheatre, with its statues of
Richelieu, Sorbon, Descartes and
Pascal and a huge allegorical
painting by Puvis de Chavannes that
covers the back wall. It has a quiet,
almost hallowed atmosphere today,
but in May 1968, this was the focal
point of the student revolt which
struck at the very roots of the French
social system.

ÉGLISE SAINT-SULPICE

Ⓜ *Saint-Sulpice*
Place Saint-Sulpice (6th)

A pious atmosphere pervades the streets of the Saint-Sulpice area, most of its little shops crammed full of rosaries, crucifixes, holy pictures and saintly statuettes. The great white church is distinguished by its strange, unmatching towers—the work of two different architects. The walls of the Chapelle des Saints-Anges are covered by frescoes painted by Delacroix between 1853 and 1861.

EIFFEL TOWER

Ⓜ *Bir-Hakeim or*
ⓇⒺⓇ *Champ de Mars*
Champ de Mars (7th)
Open daily 9.30 a.m.–midnight (winter 9.30 a.m.–11 p.m.).

The highlight of the 1889 World's Fair has become the symbol of Paris, but it was left standing only because Eiffel's estimate for dismantling his masterpiece was prohibitive. Made up of 15,000 pieces of metal fixed by 2,500,000 rivets, the tower has restaurants and tea-rooms on the two lower platforms and a lookout on the third with a view reaching 43 miles (70 km) on a clear day. The Parisians have become quite fond of their "Iron Lady" since spotlights installed inside the structure in 1985 give it an ethereal glow at night.

HÔTEL NATIONAL DES INVALIDES

Ⓜ *Varenne or* ⓇⒺⓇ *Invalides*
Esplanade des Invalides (7th)
Open daily 10 a.m.–5 p.m. (Napoleon's Tomb: 10 a.m.–7 p.m. from June to August). Closed on some public holidays.

Louis XIV founded the Invalides as the first national hospital for soldiers wounded in action. The monumental building now houses four museums, including the Army Museum, but most people come to see Napoleon's Tomb: the emperor lies directly beneath the great golden dome.

ARC DE TRIOMPHE DE L'ÉTOILE

Ⓜ *or* ⓇⒺⓇ *Charles-de-Gaulle–Etoile*
Place Charles-de-Gaulle (8th)
Open daily 9.30 a.m.–6.30 p.m.; late closing Fridays 10 p.m. (winter daily 10 a.m.–5.30 p.m.).

Napoleon's Triumphal Way culminated in his Triumphal Arch—which he never saw completed as it took 30 years to build. It now marks the half-way point between Place de la Concorde and the glistening marble Grande Arche at the Défense. Take the lift to the top to admire Baron Haussmann's geometrical town planning: 12 wide boulevards radiating out from the arch and forming a 12-pointed star. Down below, tiny cars circle round and round the arch in a never-ending stream of traffic. The remains of the Unknown Soldier were buried beneath the arch in 1920 and the eternal flame lit three years later.

ÉGLISE DE LA MADELEINE

Ⓜ *Madeleine or* Ⓡ *Auber*
Place de la Madeleine (8th)
Open daily 7 a.m.–7 p.m.; closed Sundays 1.30–3.30 p.m.

With its peristyle of Corinthian columns, the Madeleine church looks more like a displaced Parthenon. With any luck you might see a high-society wedding spilling down its grand flight of steps. Construction of the church, begun for Louis XV in 1764, was halted by the Revolution. Napoleon dithered between a bank, a theatre and a library before deciding to turn the unfinished building into a temple dedicated to his Grand Army. It was finally completed and consecrated as a Catholic church under Louis XVIII.

OPÉRA NATIONAL DE PARIS – GARNIER

Ⓜ *Opéra or* Ⓡ *Auber*
Place de l'Opéra (9th)
Open daily except Sunday 10 a.m.–6 p.m.
(winter 10 a.m.–5 p.m.). Closed in August.

The theatre built for Napoleon III is now the seat of the National Ballet.

Despite its imposing size, only 2,000 spectators fit into the circular space crowned by a ceiling painted by Chagall in 1964 and a sparkling 6-ton chandelier. The Opéra has been recently restored and reopened in early 1996.

The opera museum, 8, rue Scribe, open 10 a.m.–5 p.m., displays interesting collections of drawings, paintings, stage sets and costumes.

CATACOMBS

Ⓜ *or* Ⓡ *Denfert-Rochereau*
1, place Denfert-Rochereau (14th)
Open Tuesday to Friday 2–4 p.m.; Saturday and Sunday 9–11 a.m. and 2–4 p.m.

A grisly tour through an ancient quarry transformed into a huge underground cemetery containing the skeletons of 6 million Parisians, with their femurs, tibias and skulls arranged in artistic patterns.

TOUR MONTPARNASSE

Ⓜ *Montparnasse-Bienvenüe*
Rue de l'Arrivée (15th)
Open daily 9.30 a.m.–11.30 p.m. (winter 9.30 a.m.–10.30 p.m.).

The tall, narrow, dark tower seems to loom at the end of every perspective over the left bank. A lift whisks you up in 40 seconds to the 56th floor for one of the best panoramic views of Paris from on high.

PALAIS DE CHAILLOT AND ESPLANADE DU TROCADÉRO

Ⓜ *Trocadéro*
Place du Trocadéro (16th)

This is the place to come for your photos of the Eiffel Tower. From the terrace of the symmetrical 1930s construction the view stretches over the gardens and fountains of the Trocadéro, across the Seine, through the arch of the tower and along the Champ de Mars all the way to the elegant Ecole Militaire, with the golden dome of the Invalides and the curving UNESCO building on the horizon. A national theatre and five museums are housed in the wings of the palais de Chaillot.

BASILIQUE DU SACRÉ-CŒUR

Ⓜ *Anvers or Abbesses*
Parvis du Sacré-Cœur (18th)
Open daily 6.40 a.m.–11 p.m.
Dome and crypt 9 a.m.–6 p.m.

Its bulbous silhouette dominates the Parisian horizon as a symbol of penitence after the 1871 insurrection of the Commune. Built from a special stone that whitens with the contact of carbonic gas in the atmosphere, the basilica can be reached by a funicular that leaves from Marché Saint-Pierre (Ⓜ Anvers), or by a lengthy flight of steps. Go up to the dome for the view over the rooftops of the old village of Montmartre, which still has its own vineyard.

SAINT-PIERRE DE MONTMARTRE

Ⓜ *Abbesses*
2, rue du Mont-Cenis (18th)

More modest than its gleaming white neighbour, this old church was built in 1147 as part of a great abbey. Inside are the tombs of several abbesses, from Adelaide of Savoy, the founder, to Louise-Marie de Montmorency-Laval, beheaded during the Revolution.

GRANDE ARCHE DE LA DÉFENSE

Ⓜ *or* Ⓡ Ⓔ Ⓡ *La Défense*
1, parvis de la Défense,
92 Puteaux
Open daily from 9 a.m.–7 p.m.
(winter 9 a.m.–6 p.m.)

Clad in white and grey marble, the Grande Arche towers over the Défense business district at the end of the perspective formed by the Tuileries, Champs-Elysées and Avenue de la Grande-Armée, a colossal echo of Napoleon's Arc de Triomphe. Designed by Danish architect Johann-Otto von Spreckelsen and inaugurated in 1989 for the Bicentenary of the Revolution, this "window open onto the world" measures 360 ft (110 m) in height and 347 ft (106 m) in width. Offices fill the side walls, conference rooms occupy the roof, and bubble lifts whisk you through the network of a fibreglass "cloud" to the terrace.

13

Museums

Entrance tickets vary from around 20 to 50 F. If you intend to do a lot of museum-visiting during your stay, it might be worth investing in a Museum Pass (Carte musées et monuments), giving direct access to the permanent collections in 65 museums (i.e. no queuing!). The pass can be obtained at the Paris Tourist Office, the main métro stations and the museums and monuments themselves. Valid for one, three or five consecutive days, it costs 70, 140 and 200 F respectively.

MUSÉE NATIONAL DU LOUVRE

Ⓜ *Palais Royal–Musée du Louvre
or Louvre–Rivoli
Cour Napoléon (1st)
Open Thursday to Sunday 9 a.m.–
6 p.m.; Mondays and Wednesdays
9 a.m.–9.45 p.m. Closed Tuesday.*

If you want to enjoy the Louvre in relative peace, try to visit in the morning. Make sure you have plenty of time in hand, for the museum is far bigger than you imagine. And decide your priorities first: if you just wander aimlessly around, your brain will soon suffer from overload. Even a "highlights only" tour involves a great deal of walking. When the "new Louvre" was opened in 1993, incorporating the three floors of the Richelieu Wing, the exhibition space doubled, making this the biggest museum in the world. More than 4,000 masterpieces which had been in storage for years were brought out on display. The main entrance is beneath I.M. Pei's glass pyramid in the middle of the Cour Napoléon, but you can also enter from the rue de Rivoli, opposite the Place du Palais Royal. Pick up a floor plan at the information desk to help you find your way around the labyrinth.

The collections are grouped as follows: Greek, Etruscan and Roman Antiquities; Egyptian Antiquities; Islamic Art; Applied Arts; paintings of the French, Italian, Spanish, Dutch, Flemish, German and English schools; and sculpture—superbly displayed in the three glassed-over courtyards of the Richelieu Wing.

CENTRE NATIONAL D'ART ET DE CULTURE GEORGES POMPIDOU

Ⓜ *Rambuteau* or
Ⓡ *Châtelet-Les Halles*
Place Beaubourg (4th)
Open Monday, Wednesday, Thursday, Friday noon–10 p.m.; Saturday, Sunday and holidays 10 a.m.–10 p.m.

Better known as the Pompidou Centre, or simply Beaubourg, this very daring project of the late 70s has grown into its surroundings. Millions of visitors come here, some to see the unseemly building with all its appendages of tubes, wires, shafts and air ducts, others to watch the amazing street entertainment on the plaza, but the majority for the spectacular art exhibitions.

After extensive renovation of the façade, it is now the turn of the interior cultural areas, which will be closed for refurbishment until January 2000. However, the Museum of Modern Art on the 4th floor remains open. It displays 25,000 works of the Fauvist, Cubist, Abstract and Surrealist schools. Entrance tickets to the exhibitions are sold only at the ground-floor ticket office.

MUSÉE D'ORSAY

Ⓜ *Solférino* or Ⓡ *Musée d'Orsay*
1, rue de Bellechasse (7th)
Open 9 a.m.–6 p.m.
(winter 10 a.m.–6 p.m.). Late closing Thursday, 9.45 p.m.

In this refurbished railway station, the architecture alone is enough to take your breath away. You'll need at least three hours to see the best of the magnificent collections covering French art from 1848 to 1914: Impressionists and post-

15

Impressionists, Art Nouveau furniture, sculpture, architecture, the beginnings of photography. Pick up a plan at the entrance as it isn't too easy to find your way around. The Impressionists are on the top floor, reached by escalators hidden by great pillars at the far end of the main hall.

The restaurant, on the middle level above the entrance, is rather grand, all gold trim and chandeliers. There's a more easy-going Rooftop Café on the upper level, with an outside terrace.

CITÉ DES SCIENCES ET DE L'INDUSTRIE

Ⓜ *Porte de la Villette*
30, ave Corentin-Cariou (19th)
Open Tuesday to Saturday
10 a.m.–6 p.m.;
Sunday 10 a.m.–7 p.m.

Even if the words "science" and "industry" make you shudder, you'll enjoy this vast hands-on activity centre just as much as the children do. La Villette (four times as big as the Pompidou Centre) scrupulously avoids calling itself a museum. The permanent exhibition covers four main themes—the universe, the earth, space and the environment—in such a way as to make it all genuinely fascinating. The Cinaxe is a "moving" movie theatre; the Argonaute a real hunter submarine;

and the gleaming silver Géode, by far the biggest draw, has a hemispheric screen showing films on nature, the environment, and discovery.

❏ *OTHER MUSEUMS*

MUSÉE DES ARTS DÉCORATIFS

Ⓜ *Palais Royal–Musée du Louvre*
or ⓇⒺⓇ *Châtelet–Les Halles*
Palais du Louvre,
107, rue de Rivoli (1st)
Open Wednesday to Saturday
12.30–6 p.m.; Sunday noon–6 p.m.

Furniture, furnishings and objets d'art through the ages shown in permanent and temporary exhibitions. The museum is housed in a wing of the Louvre but has a separate entrance. Part of it is devoted to the Musée de l'Affiche et de la Publicité: posters and advertising.

MUSÉE DE L'ORANGERIE

Ⓜ *Concorde or* ⓇⒺⓇ *Invalides*
Place de la Concorde (1st)
Open daily 9.45 a.m.–5.15 p.m.
Closed Tuesday and certain public holidays.

This small museum on the river side of the Tuileries houses the delightful Walter Guillaume collection of Impressionists: Cézanne, Renoir, le Douanier Rousseau, among other early 20th-century painters. Eight peaceful water-lily murals by Monet, *les Nymphéas,* adorn the two oval ground-floor rooms.

MUSÉE DE LA PARFUMERIE FRAGONARD

Ⓜ *Opéra*
39, bd des Capucines (2nd)
Open daily 9 a.m.–6 p.m.
Admission free.

The Belle-Epoque Théâtre des Capucines, renovated in 1992, houses a fascinating museum tracing the fragrant, 3,000-year history of perfume and cosmetics. A similar museum closer to the Opéra is at 9, rue Scribe.

MUSÉE CARNAVALET

Ⓜ *Saint-Paul or*
Ⓡ *Châtelet–Les Halles*
23, rue Sévigné (3rd)
Open daily 10 a.m.–5.40 p.m.
Closed Monday and
public holidays.

The handsome 16th-century town house of compulsive epistle-writer Mme de Sévigné was converted into a museum in 1880 and extended to a neighbouring mansion in 1989. It retraces the history of Paris from its beginnings to modern times.

MUSÉE COGNACQ-JAY

Ⓜ *Saint-Paul*
8, rue Elzévir (3rd)
Open daily 10 a.m.–5.40 p.m.
Closed Monday.

Ernest Cognacq and Louise Jay founded the department store La Samaritaine. They bequeathed their collection of 18th-century paintings to the city of Paris: delicate works by Fragonard, Chardin and Boucher. Plus furniture and ceramics.

MUSÉE PICASSO

Ⓜ *Saint-Paul*
5, rue de Thorigny (3rd)
Open daily 9.30 a.m.–6 p.m.
(winter 9.30 a.m.–5 p.m.)

The 17th-century Hôtel Salé makes a handsome setting for Picasso's personal collection of paintings made up of works by Matisse, Cézanne, Miró and Renoir, plus his own paintings and sculpture, photographs and documents.

MAISON DE VICTOR HUGO

Ⓜ *Bastille*
Hôtel de Rohan-Guéménée,
6, place des Vosges (4th)
Open daily 10 a.m.–5.40 p.m.
Closed Monday and
public holidays.

Victor Hugo lived in this cosy seven-room apartment from 1833 to 1848. He wrote a few chapters of *Les Misérables* here, and filled in his spare time by making some of the furniture. His drawings, letters and manuscripts are on display.

INSTITUT DU MONDE ARABE

Ⓜ *Jussieu* or Ⓡ *Gare d'Austerlitz*
1, rue des Fossés–St-Bernard (5th)
Open 10 a.m.–6 p.m. Closed
Monday.

Art and literature of the Arab world from the 8th to 19th centuries, in an ultra-modern glass and aluminium building. The windows open and close automatically with the variation in light, like a camera shutter.

MUSÉE NATIONAL DU MOYEN-ÂGE–THERMES DE CLUNY

Ⓜ *Cluny-La Sorbonne* or
Ⓡ *Saint-Michel*
6, place Paul-Painlevé (5th)
Open daily 9.15 a.m.–5.45 p.m.
Closed Tuesday and public
holidays.

The remains of the Gallo-Roman thermal baths form part of this building, a 15th-century mansion housing a marvellous collection of medieval sculpture, stained glass, bronzes and tapestries—of which the highlight is the series depicting *The Lady and the Unicorn*.

MUSÉE DE SCULPTURE EN PLEIN AIR

Ⓜ *Gare d'Austerlitz*
Quai Saint-Bernard (5th)
Admission free.

Contemporary sculpture is shown on a two-year rotation basis in this little park on the banks of the Seine.

MUSÉUM D'HISTOIRE NATURELLE

Ⓜ *Gare d'Austerlitz* or *Jussieu*
Jardin des Plantes (5th)
Open daily 10 a.m.–5 p.m.
Closed Tuesday and certain
public holidays.

The botanical gardens were created by Louis XIII for the cultivation of medicinal plants. The Natural History Museum is divided into several sections: mineralogy and geology (fascinating meteorites); paleontology (dinosaur skeletons); anatomy; and the new department of evolution, which explains the mystery of life. The magnificent Grande Gallerie, in glass and iron, contains a splendid collection of rare and extinct species.

MUSÉE RODIN

Ⓜ *Varenne* or Ⓡ *Invalides*
77, rue de Varenne (7th)
Open daily 9.30 a.m.–5.45 p.m.
(winter 9.30 a.m.–4.45 p.m.).
Closed Monday and public
holidays.

18th-century town house and garden providing the perfect setting for some of Rodin's finest sculptures.

GRAND PALAIS

Ⓜ *Champs-Elysées–Clemenceau*
Ave du Général-Eisenhower (8th)
Open Monday, Thursday to
Sunday 10 a.m.–8 p.m.;
Wednesday 10 a.m.–10 p.m.

A Belle Epoque palace built for the 1900 World's Fair, now used for popular temporary exhibitions.

MUSÉE CERNUSCHI

(M) *Villiers or Monceau*
7, ave Velasquez (8th)
Open daily 10 a.m.–5.40 p.m.
Closed Monday and public holidays.

A magnificent collection of Chinese art from its origins to the 13th century, together with contemporary Chinese paintings.

MUSÉE JACQUEMART-ANDRÉ

(M) *Saint-Philippe-du-Roule*
158, bd Haussmann (8th)
Open daily 10 a.m.–6 p.m.

Paintings and sculpture of the Italian Renaissance and works by European artists of the 17th and 18th centuries in a newly renovated mansion. The collection includes works by Botticelli, Chardin, Fragonard, Mantegna, Rembrandt, and frescoes by Tiepolo.

MUSÉE NISSIM DE CAMONDO

(M) *Villiers*
63, rue de Monceau (8th)
Open Wednesday to Sunday 10 a.m.–5 p.m.

An elegant 18th-century mansion, furnished with antiques, tapestries, and paintings by Mme Vigée-Lebrun and Hubert Robert.

MUSÉE DU PETIT PALAIS

(M) *Champs-Elysées–Clemenceau* or (RER) *Charles de Gaulle–Etoile*
Avenue Winston Churchill (8th)
Open daily 10 a.m.–5.40 p.m.
Closed Monday.

Paintings, sculpture, furniture, tapestries and objets d'art, the most remarkable being the late 19th-century works by Courbet, Bonnard, Pissaro, Monet and Vuillard.

PALAIS DE LA DÉCOUVERTE

(M) *Champs-Elysées–Clemenceau* or (RER) *Invalides*
Avenue Franklin-Roosevelt (8th)
Open Tuesday to Saturday 9.30 a.m.–6 p.m.; Sunday 10 a.m.–7 p.m. Closed Monday and public holidays.

In a wing of the Grand Palais, the "Palace of Discovery" makes science seem like fun. Children love the Planetarium.

MUSÉE GRÉVIN

(M) *Rue Montmartre*
10, bd Montmartre (9th)
Open daily 1 to 7 p.m.; school holidays 10 a.m.–7 p.m.

Among more than 500 wax characters preserved for posterity: a bewigged little Mozart fingers the keyboard, Hitchcock in a pensive mood reads his newspaper opposite the Invisible Man, Marilyn holds down her flyaway skirt.

MUSÉE NATIONAL DES ARTS D'AFRIQUE ET D'OCÉANIE

Ⓜ *Porte Dorée*
293, ave Daumesnil (12th)
Open weekdays 10 a.m.–noon and 1.30–5.30 p.m.; Saturday and Sunday 12.30–6 p.m. Closed Tuesday.

The art of Africa, Australia and the Pacific Islands in an Art Deco building, plus a tropical aquarium.

MUSÉE D'ART MODERNE DE LA VILLE DE PARIS

Ⓜ *Alma-Marceau* or
Ⓡ *Pont de l'Alma*
11, ave du Président-Wilson (16th)
Open daily 10 a.m.–5.30 p.m., Saturday and Sunday 10 a.m.–7 p.m. Closed Monday and public holidays.

20th-century artworks: murals by Sonia and Robert Delaunay, Matisse, and the biggest painting in the world, *La Fée Electricité* by Dufy.

MUSÉE DES ARTS ASIATIQUES – GUIMET

Ⓜ *Iéna* or Ⓡ *Pont de l'Alma*
6, place d'Iéna (16th)
Open daily 9.45 a.m.–6 p.m. Closed Tuesday.

While the museum is undergoing renovation (until end 1998), visit the peaceful Chinese and Japanese Buddhist pantheon, 19, ave d'Iéna (same hours).

MUSÉE DE L'HOMME

Ⓜ *Trocadéro*
Palais de Chaillot
17, place du Trocadéro (16th)
Open daily 9.45 a.m.–5.15 p.m. Closed Tuesday and public holidays.

The museum of mankind, presenting ethnological, anthropological and prehistoric collections from 250,000 BC to the present. Jewellery, masks, and an Easter Island statue.

MUSÉE MARMOTTAN

Ⓜ *La Muette*
2, rue Louis-Boilly (16th)
Open daily 10 a.m.–5 p.m. Closed Monday, 1 May and 25 December.

In a splendid 19th-century mansion, objets d'art and furniture of the Renaissance, Consulat and Empire periods, and an exceptional collection of Impressionist paintings (Gauguin, Sisley, Pisarro, Renoir), and 100 works by Claude Monet bequeathed by his son.

MUSÉE DE LA MODE ET DU COSTUME

Ⓜ *Iéna*
10, ave Pierre-Iᵉʳ-de-Serbie (16th)
Open daily 10 a.m.–5.40 p.m. Closed Monday and public holidays.

A recently refurbished collection of clothing illustrating changing fashion through the ages.

The Street Scene

Wander off the beaten tourist track to discover the passages and parks, the squares and neighbourhoods that give Paris its distinctive charm.

❏ *ARCADES*

The French call them *passages* or *galeries*, these covered streets where 19th-century ladies could do their shopping, go to the theatre, meet their friends and drink hot chocolate without getting the hems of their long skirts muddy. Many arcades suffered badly from neglect until recent years when they suddenly came back into fashion. Now restored, they are great places for window-shopping. Most of them are in the sector defined by the Grands Boulevards, ave de l'Opéra, rue de Rivoli and bd de Sébastopol.

GALERIE VÉRO-DODAT

Ⓜ *Louvre-Rivoli*
19, rue J.-J. Rousseau to
2, rue du Bouloi (1st)
Named after the two pork butchers who founded it in 1824, this chic shopping arcade has mahogany

shop-fronts, painted ceilings and black-and-white tiled floor.

GALERIE VIVIENNE

Ⓜ *Bourse*
4, rue des Petits-Champs to
6, rue Vivienne (2nd)

Behind the gardens of the Palais Royal, this L-shaped arcade, linked with the Galerie Colbert, was declared a national historic monument in 1974. A hallowed atmosphere pervades the corridors beneath its arched, sculpted ceiling, making an eccentric setting for fashion whizz-kid Jean-Paul Gaultier's startling designs (his windows give onto rue Vivienne). At the other end, the charming Brasserie is frequented by brokers from the nearby stock exchange.

PASSAGE DU CAIRE

Ⓜ *Sentier*
2, place du Caire to
33, rue d'Alexandrie (2nd)

Sentier is synonymous with the rag trade. There's something of the souk in the "Cairo arcade", full of inexpensive clothes shops.

PASSAGE DU GRAND-CERF

Ⓜ *Etienne-Marcel*
145, rue Saint-Denis to
10, rue Dussoubs (2nd)

Restored recently, with resplendent wood panelling on its three floors.

PASSAGE DES PANORAMAS

Ⓜ *Montmartre*
16, rue Saint-Marc to
1, bd Montmartre (2nd)

Opened in 1800 and recently restored, this arcade was named after the panoramic views painted onto a circular wall.

PASSAGE DES PRINCES

Ⓜ *Richelieu-Drouot*
5, bd des Italiens to
97, rue de Richelieu (2nd)

A tiny arcade in Napoleon III style, with renovated ironwork and tiled floor.

PASSAGE JOUFFROY

Ⓜ *Richelieu-Drouot*
10, bd Montmartre to
9, rue de la Grange-Batelière (9th)

This arcade was never allowed to become shabby, as it shelters the Musée Grévin entrance. It was the first to have central heating: hot air blown through grids in the floor.

❏ BRIDGES

Linking left bank and right, riveting the islands to the quays, Paris's bridges all have a story to tell. Following the river downstream, from the stern of the Ile de la Cité to the Pont Mirabeau, here are the bridges most worthy of attention.

The **Pont de l'Archevêché** (1828) offers a striking view of Notre-Dame. It leads to Pont Saint-Louis, usually overrun with street musicians and portrait painters.

The **Pont-Neuf** (1605) was the first to be built without houses, and despite its name (*Neuf* means new) is the oldest bridge in Paris.

Pedestrians-only **Passerelle des Arts** (1804, rebuilt in steel in 1982) is furnished with benches and potted plants, to make the view of Notre-Dame even more pleasant.

The **Pont de la Concorde** (1791) was built with stones taken from the Bastille prison, dismantled during the Revolution.

A single steel arch spanning the Seine, **Pont Alexandre III** (1900) is definitely the most romantic of the Parisian bridges, especially at night under the glow of its Belle Epoque lamps. The melodramatic statues represent Fame and Pegasus.

The **Pont de l'Alma** (1856) is known especially for its statue of the *Zouave* by Diébolt, which acts as a marker for the water level.

Cross over the **Pont d'Iéna** (1913) for a good view of the Trocadéro in one direction, the Eiffel Tower and Champ de Mars in the other.

From the **Pont Mirabeau** (1897) you can see the original Statue of Liberty, standing proudly in front of the Pont de Grenelle.

❏ SQUARES

PLACE DAUPHINE
Ⓜ *Pont-Neuf*
(1st) The red-brick façades of imposing 17th-century apartment buildings form an elegant triangle.

PLACE VENDOME
Ⓜ *Opéra*
(1st) A prestigious address for most of the capital's jewellers. Napoleon Bonaparte, dressed as Caesar, watches all the action from his perch on the central column.

PLACE DES VOSGES
Ⓜ *Chemin-Vert*
(4th) A study in harmony and symmetry, featuring 36 red-brick houses around a peaceful garden. Beneath the arcades: arty boutiques, galleries, cafés and restaurants.

PLACE IGOR STRAVINSKY
Ⓜ *Hôtel de Ville*
(4th) There's always something going on in the big square fronting

the "Pompidou Centre" at Beaubourg. You can spend hours watching sword-swallowers, fire-eaters, rappers and drummers, have your hair plaited, your name inscribed on a grain of rice, or just sit and eat a sandwich and contemplate Niki de Saint-Phalle's mobile sculptures in the fountain.

PLACE DE LA CONCORDE
Ⓜ *Concorde*
(8th) See it at night, when the traffic has died down and the fountains are illuminated. The pink granite obelisk from the temple of Ramses II in Louxor dates from 1300 BC. It was set up here in 1836, as a gift from Mohammed Ali, viceroy of Egypt.

PLACE DU TERTRE
Ⓜ *Abbesses*
(18th) The "village square" of old Montmartre, giving picturesque perspectives of the domes of the Sacré-Cœur. If you want to be immortalized in charcoal, the street artists will oblige, at a price!

❏ *PARKS AND GARDENS*

JARDIN DES TUILERIES
Ⓜ *Palais-Royal*
Place de la Concorde (1st)
Open 9.45 a.m.–5 p.m. Closed Tuesday.

The king's gardener, Le Nôtre, designed the vast Tuileries gardens in 1649. The famous female nude statues by Aristide Maillol (1861–1944) are grouped in the Carrousel part of the gardens, nearest to the Louvre.

JARDINS DU PALAIS-ROYAL
Ⓜ *Palais-Royal*
Place du Palais-Royal (1st)
Buren's black and white striped columns (1986) in the first courtyard are a favourite with children who jump on and off; you can always find one that's just the right height for a seat. The garden with sandpit, rosebeds, fountains and fragrant avenues of lime trees is a secluded retreat only seconds away from the roaring traffic. Beneath the arcades, the tea rooms and shops selling antiques, old books and prints, tin soldiers and wooden toys are utterly genteel—a far cry from 18th-century days when the Palais-Royal was riddled with gambling dens.

JARDIN DES HALLES
ⓇⒺⓇ *Châtelet-Les Halles*
Rue Berger (1st)
Closed Monday and rainy days.
A bamboo forest, marshland and exotic plants fill this greenhouse. The Jardin des Enfants aux Halles (105, rue Rambuteau, 3rd) is a playschool for children from

7 to 11; you can leave yours here to explore the jungle while you do your shopping in the nearby Forum.

JARDIN DU LUXEMBOURG

Ⓜ *Luxembourg*
Boulevard Saint-Michel (6th)

Beautifully dressed French children sail their little boats on the pond in this formal garden, where mossy statues drowse beneath chestnut trees and students ponder the meaning of life between lectures.

PARC MONCEAU

Ⓜ *Monceau*
58, bd Courcelles (8th)

The 18th-century version of an English park, dotted with romantic follies such as Greek-looking ruins and a decrepit Gothic castle.

PARC FLORAL DE PARIS

Ⓜ *Château de Vincennes*
Esplanade du Château de Vincennes (12th)
Open daily 9.30 a.m.– 6 or 8 p.m. (winter 9.30 a.m.–5 p.m.).

Flowers, lawns, a picnic area, and plenty to keep the children happy.

PARC MONTSOURIS

Ⓜ *Cité Universitaire*
Boulevard Jourdan (14th)

Former wasteland and quarries transformed into a recreation ground by Baron Haussmann. Relaxed atmosphere, with hills and grotto, waterfall, statues, majestic trees and an incongruous reproduction of the Bardo palace of Tunis.

PARC ANDRÉ CITROËN

Ⓜ *Balard*
Rue Balard (15th)

An unusual park built on the site of the old Citroën factory. Sections on various themes—white garden, black garden, Mediterranean flora and an orange grove.

BOIS DE BOULOGNE

Ⓜ *Porte Maillot, Porte Dauphine or Porte d'Auteuil*

This huge forest on the western edge of the city is laced with cycle paths and horse trails. Also boating lakes, restaurants, cafés and Longchamp and Auteuil race courses. After 8 p.m. it is closed and strictly out of bounds.
In the Parc de Bagatelle, 700 rose varieties bloom in summer.

JARDIN D'ACCLIMATATION

Ⓜ *Les Sablons*
Bois de Boulogne (16th)
Open daily 10 a.m.–6 p.m.
Admission fee.

A miniature train, merry-go-rounds, theatre, puppet show, mini-golf, pony rides, a farm and the Musée en Herbe (nature museum) make this a delightful place to take the children.

❏ *NEIGHBOURHOODS*

LE MARAIS

(3rd & 4th) The sector enclosed by rues Beaubourg and Turbigo, boulevard Beaumarchais, and rues de Rivoli and Saint-Antoine is a treasure chest of 17th-century architecture. Many of the mansions have been turned into museums. The Marais has become a trendy district, crowded at weekends but pleasantly quiet otherwise, with art galleries, boutiques, antique shops, tea rooms, restaurants and gay bars.

ÎLE SAINT-LOUIS

(4th) Shown on ancient maps as cow pasture, the quiet island is now one of the most stylish places to live. Visit the elegant church of Saint-Louis-en-l'Île, window-shop the chic boutiques, wander along the quais, and don't forget to try one of Berthillon's fabulous ice creams.

QUARTIER SAINT-SÉVERIN

(5th) The narrow, medieval streets in the block formed by boulevards Saint-Michel, Saint-Germain, rue Saint-Jacques and quai Saint-Michel are for pedestrians only, packed with tourists day and night. The restaurants have names like Aphrodite, Naxos and Plaka and the aroma of spit-roast lamb and kebabs wafts round the corners.

SAINT-GERMAIN-DES-PRÉS

(6th) Cinemas, designer boutiques, cafés and bookshops are hallmarks of boulevard Saint-Germain, at its most lively around the old church of the same name. The romantic, literary aura of the Saint-Germain of the 1950s has long drifted the same way as Jean-Paul Sartre and his existentialist disciples, but if you wander the narrow streets between the boulevard and the river—rue de Seine, Saint-André-des-Arts, rue de l'Echaudé, rue Christine, place Furstenberg—you'll sense the rare, authentic "Parisian" atmosphere.

MONTPARNASSE

(6th) This largely commercial and residential area marking the outer limits of the Latin Quarter has undergone drastic changes since it was the haunt of poets, singers and philosophers in pre-war years. Their cafés remain, Closerie des Lilas and La Coupole, where people still go to see and be seen.

CHINATOWN

(13th) For an exotic change of scenery, visit the streets between place d'Italie and porte de Choisy where, in the 70s, thousands of refugees from Cambodia, Laos, Vietnam, Thailand and China settled in the then spanking new tower blocks. On Sundays, the whole

Asiatic population of Paris homes in on the huge Chinese supermarkets and open-air stalls.

MONTMARTRE

(18th) A little vineyard on the corner of rue Saint-Vincent and rue des Saules remains from the time when Montmartre really was a village. Still self-enclosed, the area is beseiged with tourists in search of "Gay Paree". If you leave place du Tertre and explore the residential streets, you'll find splendid villas, artist's studios (look for the big windows) and quiet squares. The Bateau-Lavoir studio on Place Emile-Goudeau, where Picasso, Braque and Juan Gris developed Cubism, has been replaced by a complex of studios, but photos in the windows show the squalid conditions in which those artists once worked.

BELLEVILLE

(20th) From Turkey, Africa, the Caribbean and Asia, around 50 different nationalities jostle in the streets of Belleville, an ebullient neighbourhood with the most exotic street markets imaginable.

❏ CEMETERIES

They all have the same opening hours: summer 8 a.m. to 8 p.m.; winter 8 a.m. to 5.30 p.m.

CIMETIÈRE DU MONTPARNASSE

Ⓜ *Edgar Quinet or Raspail*
Boulevard Edgar-Quinet (14th)
Among the distinguished residents of this peaceful cemetery, Guy de Maupassant, Baudelaire, Simone de Beauvoir and Jean-Paul Sartre.

CIMETIÈRE DE MONTMARTRE

Ⓜ *Place de Clichy*
Avenue Rachel (18th)
The last resting place of Degas, Stendhal, Berlioz, Alfred de Vigny, and, in more recent years, the popular singer Dalida who lived in Montmartre.

CIMETIÈRE DU PÈRE-LACHAISE

Ⓜ *Philippe Auguste*
16, rue du Repos (20th)
Since Jim Morrison of the Doors was buried here in 1971, this has become the most visited cemetery in the world. Every day, a stream of teenage admirers come to light a candle or lay a memento on his tomb, leaving a trail of graffiti in their wake. A million people are buried here; the best way to find the tombs of the famous—Chopin, Delacroix, Oscar Wilde, Simone Signoret, Edith Piaf and too many more—is to buy a map at the entrance. If you speak French, it's well worth investing in a guided tour, listed under "Conférences" in *Pariscope* and the newspapers.

$shopping$

In general, food shops are open from Tuesday to Saturday from 9 a.m.–1 p.m. and 4–7 p.m. Some open on Sunday mornings. Boutiques open Tuesday to Saturday 9.30 a.m.–6.30 p.m. and Monday 2.30–6.30 p.m. The department stores all have one evening per week for late closing.

❏ DEPARTMENT STORES

LA SAMARITAINE
Ⓜ Pont-Neuf
. 19, rue de la Monnaie (1st)
Late shopping until 10 p.m.
Wednesday. Closed Monday.
As the slogan goes: "You can find everything at La Samaritaine". The work clothes department is reputed.

BAZAR DE L'HÔTEL DE VILLE (B.H.V.)
Ⓜ Hôtel-de-Ville
52–64, rue de Rivoli (4th)
Late shopping until 10 p.m.
Wednesday.
Irresistible selection of doorknobs, brass keyholes, curtain rings and fabrics in the home furnishings department.

AU BON MARCHÉ

Ⓜ *Sèvres-Babylone*
38, rue de Sèvres (7th)
Excellent food department (Grande Epicerie de Paris, magasin 2, ground floor), open 8.30 a.m.–8.30 p.m. (till 2 a.m. Friday). French specialities, a wide range of wines, good cooked foods *(service traiteur)*.

GALERIES LAFAYETTE

Ⓜ *Chaussée d'Antin*
40, bd Haussmann (9th)
Perfumes, cosmetics, lingerie, handbags, kitchenware, home furnishings, electric fittings, and all the great names in French fashion. Spectacular circular galleries under a huge stained-glass dome.

MARKS & SPENCER

Ⓜ *Chaussée d'Antin*
35, bd Haussmann (9th)
Where French housewives come for "classic" sweaters and English scones. Another, new, branch at 88, rue de Rivoli.

PRINTEMPS

Ⓜ *Havre-Caumartin*
64, bd Haussmann (9th)
Good for trendy young fashions, big perfume department and excellent choice of kitchenware and stationery. The stained-glass cupola over the "Espace Flo" restaurant is a listed monument.

❏ *SHOPPING CENTRES*

CARROUSEL DU LOUVRE

Ⓜ *Louvre*
Musée du Louvre (1st)
The marble-clad underground gallery beneath the Rond-Point du Carrousel has a number of up-market boutiques, including the Louvre gift shop and a Virgin Megastore, plus several self-service restaurants. You can see part of the medieval city walls, uncovered during the excavations. Special exhibitions and the big designer fashion shows are held down here.

FORUM DES HALLES

Ⓜ *Les Halles*
1–7, rue Pierre-Lescot (1st)
All the main chain stores have a branch in this slightly tacky temple to commercialism, built on sunken levels. Video monitors help you find your way around.

DRUGSTORE PUBLICIS

Ⓜ *Charles-de-Gaulle–Etoile*
133, ave des Champs-Elysées (8th);
Ⓜ *Franklin D. Roosevelt*
1, ave Matignon (8th)
Open daily 9 a.m.–2 a.m.,
Sundays too.
Much more than a drugstore: it includes fashion boutiques, grocery stores, tobacconists, newsagents, toyshops, restaurants, and so on.

HAUTE COUTURE

The big names in designer fashion tend to cluster together in certain areas of the city. Wander along rue du Faubourg Saint-Honoré, avenue Montaigne, avenue Victor Hugo or avenue George-V to compare the creations of Pierre Cardin, Chanel, Dior, Hermès, Christian Lacroix, Lanvin, Nina Ricci, Saint Laurent, and so on. Many of the younger designers have taken premises close to the Palais Royal and the Bibliothèque nationale in grand 18th-century buildings: Chantal Thomass at 1, rue Vivienne; Jean-Paul Gaultier in the Galerie Vivienne; Kenzo, Stéphane Kélian, Thierry Mugler on Place des Victoires.

❏ GOURMET SHOPS

Who sells the freshest bread? Or the ripest cheeses? Where's the best place to go for wines? In Paris you are spoiled for choice.

COMPAGNIE ANGLAISE DES THÉS

Ⓜ *Les Halles*
Forum des Halles
1, rue Pierre Lescot (1st)
The English Tea Company offers more kinds of tea than you could ever imagine, sold loose from shiny scarlet tins. And if you came to Paris without your tea-strainer, you'll find one here, along with fruitcake, shortbread, gingersnaps and other British goodies.

FLO PRESTIGE

Ⓜ *Pyramides*
42, place du Marché Saint-Honoré (1st)
Open daily 8 a.m.–11 p.m.
Take-away service: mixed salads, pâtés and terrines, cooked dishes, bread, wines and spirits.

LA GALERIE DES VINS

Ⓜ *Pyramides*
201, rue Saint-Honoré (1st)
A cellar full of surprises, from local wines *(vins de pays)* to some of the most prestigious labels.

AU PANETIER

Ⓜ *Bourse*
10, Place des Petits-Pères (2nd)
Closed Saturday and Sunday
Belle Epoque décor for this bakery complete with old brick oven. Crusty baguettes and delicious farmhouse bread *(pain de campagne)* baked on a wood fire—ask for a Saint Fiacre.

REPAIRE DE BACCHUS

Ⓜ *Sentier*
88, rue Montorgueil (2nd);
Ⓜ *Monge*
112, rue Mouffetard (5th)
A wide range of good-quality wines.

BERTHILLON

Ⓜ *Pont Marie*
31, rue Saint-Louis-en-l'Ile (4th)
Open Wednesday to Sunday
10 a.m.–8 p.m. Closed July and
August.

Fancy a gingerbread ice cream? Or a mango sorbet? Join the queue outside Berthillon, you're in for a treat.

L'ÉPICERIE DU MONDE

Ⓜ *Hôtel de Ville*
30, rue François-Miron (4th)
Closed Sunday and Monday.

Not only spices, but also rice, beans, jams, olives and rum—flavours from all over the world jostle for place in this fragrant little shop.

JO GOLDENBERG

Ⓜ *Saint-Paul*
7 &15, rue des Rosiers (4th)

Renowned restaurant and takeaway, with French and Yiddish specialities.

MARIAGE FRÈRES

Ⓜ *Hôtel de Ville*
30–32, rue du Bourg-Tibourg (4th);
Ⓜ *Saint-Michel*
13, rue des Grands-Augustins (6th)
Open daily 10.30 a.m.–7 p.m.

You feel like lowering your voice when you enter this very chic shop specializing in tea. Delicately flavoured leaves for all tastes, tea sets, tea-flavoured chocolate and tea jelly for your morning toast.

SACHA FINKELSZTAJN

Ⓜ *Saint-Paul*
27, rue des Rosiers (4th)
Open Wednesday to Sunday,
10 a.m.–2 p.m. and 3–7 p.m.

This Jewish bakery's poppy-seed strudel is irresistible.

VIALARD

Ⓜ *Monge*
14, rue Monge (5th)
Open Wednesday to Sunday,
7 a.m.–8 p.m.

A Rococo setting for crusty loaves of bread in many shapes and flavours, and luscious cakes.

BRÛLERIE DE L'ODÉON

Ⓜ *Odéon*
6, rue Crébillon (6th)
Closed Sunday and Monday.

In this lovely old shop they've been roasting coffee beans since 1853. Apart from delectable coffee, you'll find all you need for brewing it.

POILÂNE

Ⓜ *Sèvres-Babylone*
8, rue du Cherche-Midi (6th);
Ⓜ *Sèvres-Babylone*
49, bd de Grenelle (15th)
Open Tuesday to Sunday
7.15 a.m.–8.15 p.m.

With his loaves of stone-ground flour and sea salt, Lionel Poilâne has become a legend in the merciless world of French bread-lovers.

31

AMANDINE

Ⓜ *Latour-Maubourg*
178, rue de Grenelle (7th)
An excellent bakery which takes special pride in its varied choice of sandwiches.

ANNE-MARIE CANTIN

Ⓜ *Ecole Militaire*
12, rue du Champ-de-Mars (7th)
Tuesday to Saturday
8.30 a.m.– 7.30 p.m., and Sunday
8.30 a.m.–4 p.m.
This lady knows all there is to know about cheese. You can visit the cellars where the big cheeses are maturing (afternoons only; book the previous day, tel. 01 45 50 43 94), and even join in one of their cheese-tastings (*dégustation*).

AUX DÉLICES DE GRENELLE

Ⓜ *La Motte Picquet-Grenelle*
206, rue de Grenelle (7th)
Open daily 11 a.m.–2.30 p.m.
and 4.30–9 p.m.
Extra-special Chinese takeaway.

COFFEE HAS-BEAN

Ⓜ *Falguière*
131, rue du Cherche-Midi (7th)
Homesick North Americans can stock up here on peanut butter, maple syrup, and, of course, coffee of all kinds, freshly roasted on the premises.

LE CHOCOLAT PAR MICHEL CHAUDUN

Ⓜ *Invalides*
149, rue de l'Université (7th)
Chocoholics beware. Just one whiff of the magical aroma wafting through the door and you're hooked.

ANDROUET

Ⓜ *Liège*
41, rue d'Amsterdam (8th)
Open Monday to Saturday
10 a.m.–7 p.m.
More than 200 different kinds of cheese, matured on the spot.

CAVES DE LA MADELEINE

Ⓜ *Madeleine*
Cité Berryer,
25, rue Royale (8th)
Wines from all regions, including an enormous choice of the best French vintages.

DALLOYAU

Ⓜ *Saint-Philippe-du-Roule*
99, rue du Faubourg
Saint-Honoré (8th)
Other branches in the 2nd, 6th,
7th and 15th arrondissements.
A Parisian institution: cold meats, pâtés, salads and cooked dishes to take away. Delicious macaroons.

FAUCHON

Ⓜ *Madeleine*
26, place de la Madeleine (8th)

The ultimate in luxury foodstores, famed for its window displays.

GRAND'MÈRE L'OYE

Ⓜ *Anvers*
57, rue de Dunkerque (9th)
"Old Mother Goose" sells all kinds of goosey products: foie gras, rillettes, preserved goose (confit), tins of goose fat, all guaranteed free from artificial additives.

LA MAISON DU CHOCOLAT

Ⓜ *Madeleine*
8, bd de la Madeleine (9th)
Tantalizing home-made chocolates, marrons glacés, macaroons and other delights.

TARTE JULIE

Ⓜ *Madeleine*
12, rue Vignon (9th)
Open daily except Sunday,
9.30 a.m.–7.30 p.m.
Sweet and savoury tarts, salads, pizzas, to take away or enjoy on the spot.

LUCULLUS D'AUTEUIL

Ⓜ *Michel-Ange Auteuil*
55, rue d'Auteuil (16th)
Closed Monday.
The affluent residents of the 16th arrondissement buy their takeaways at Lucullus: tasty, long-simmered dishes in the true bourgeois tradition.

BOUQUINISTES

As you walk along the river banks, browse through the boxes of the bouquinistes, stretching from Ile St-Louis to the Tuileries, on both sides of the Seine. Though their name comes from *bouquin,* slang for book, the dealers do not only dabble in second-hand and anti-quarian books, but also old maga-zines, postcards, stamps, old coins, engravings, posters, and nowadays, inevitable miniature Arcs de Triomphe and Eiffel Towers. The tradition began in 1539, when travelling salesmen were prohibited from peddling their wares from door to door. Granted the right to sell old books in 1859, the bouquinistes enjoyed a life free of bureaucratic restric-tions until 1994, when new regula-tions were passed, imposing registration and license fees, and forbidding the sale of anything considered to be lacking in "artis-tic merit".

LE STÜBLI

Ⓜ *Ternes*
11, rue Poncelet (17th)
Open Tuesday to Saturday
8.30 a.m.–7.30 p.m., and
Sunday morning.
If you fancy a little something along the lines of a Sachertorte or an apple strudel, visit this pâtisserie.

❏ *MARKETS*

Every arrondissement has at least one food market, open two or three days a week (never on a Monday), from 7 a.m. to 1 p.m. Even if you don't want to stock up on fruit and veg, they are a delight to wander around. Here is a small selection, in addition to the more specialized markets where you can rummage among old clothes, buy a canary or fall for an antique.

MARCHÉ DU TEMPLE
Ⓜ *Temple*
rues Eugène Spuller, Dupetit-Thouars and Perrée (3rd)
Tuesday to Friday 9 a.m.–noon (boutiques until 7 p.m.), Saturday and Sunday 9 a.m. to 1 p.m.
Boutiques and stalls filled with racks and heaps of clothes.

MARCHÉ AUX FLEURS
Ⓜ *Cité*
Place Louis-Lépine (4th)
Daily except Sunday
10 a.m.–7 p.m.
A flower and plant market, in front of the Palais de Justice.

MARCHÉ AUX OISEAUX
Ⓜ *Cité*
Place Louis-Lépine (4th)
Sundays only, 8 a.m.–7 p.m.
Turning to song, the flower market becomes a bird market on Sundays.

MARCHÉ MAUBERT
Ⓜ *Maubert-Mutualité*
Place Maubert (5th)
Tuesdays, Thursdays and Saturdays 7.30 a.m.–1.30 p.m.
Good open-air food market.

MARCHÉ MOUFFETARD
Ⓜ *Monge*
Rue Mouffetard (5th)
On medieval maps of Paris, rue Mouffetard meanders far out into the countryside. It still has lots of character, with a colourful market every morning.

MARCHÉ BIOLOGIQUE
Ⓜ *Rennes*
Boulevard Raspail (6th)
Sundays 7 a.m.–1.30 p.m.
On the boulevard between rues de Cherche-Midi and de Rennes, organically grown or reared produce.

MARCHÉ SAINT-GERMAIN
Ⓜ *Mabillon*
3ᵉʳ rue Mabillon (6th)
Tuesday to Saturday 8 a.m.–1 p.m., 6–7.30 p.m.; Sunday, mornings only.
Large covered food market.

MARCHÉ AUX TIMBRES
Ⓜ *Champs-Elysées-Clemenceau*
Cours Marigny (8th)
Thursday, Saturday, Sunday and holidays, 10 a.m.–6 p.m.

The philatelists' rendez-vous has expanded to include phonecards and other modern-day collectables.

MARCHÉ BASTILLE

Ⓜ *Bastille or Bréguet Sabin*
Boulevard Richard Lenoir (11th)
Thursday and Sunday,
7 a.m.–1.30 p.m.

Everything from live crabs to sewing machines is sold in this cheerful street market. The stalls are set along the central area of the boulevard, covering the Canal Saint-Martin. You can peek through big holes (called *oculi*) and see the barges passing below.

MARCHÉ BEAUVAU
SAINT-ANTOINE

Ⓜ *Ledru-Rollin*
Place d'Aligre (12th)
Daily except Sunday and Monday
7.30 a.m.–1 p.m.

Food, jumble and old clothes in the square and on rue d'Aligre.

MARCHÉ AUX PUCES

Ⓜ *Porte de Clignancourt or Porte*
de Saint-Ouen
Porte de Saint-Ouen (18th)
Open Saturday to Monday,
7.30 a.m.– 7 p.m.

The famous fleamarket is made up of six distinct markets, covering the whole range from *brocante* (second-hand goods) to *antiquités*

(the real thing). It's best to get there early in the day.

Paul-Bert for country-style furniture, antique dolls, bistro-type tables and chairs.

Biron is more bourgeois, dealing in genuine antiques.

Malik for clothes, all styles and all prices.

Serpette, the trendiest, mainly early 20th-century furniture.

Jules-Vallès, the cheapest. If you're lucky, you might nose out a treasure among the heaps of junk.

Vernaison, founded in 1920. Specializes in furniture, ornaments and silverware.

MARCHÉ DU LIVRE ANCIEN ET D'OCCASION

Ⓜ *Porte de Vanves*
Parc Georges Brassens, Porte
Brancion
Saturday and Sunday
9 a.m.–6 p.m.

Antiquarian and second-hand books, in a cast-iron building salvaged from the old Halles central market. With time and patience you may find a treasure, but you can also buy books by the kilo to fill up your shelves.

❏ *ANTIQUES*

Whether you're a discriminating amateur of Boulle commodes or an inveterate collector of kitsch, you're bound to find something tantalizing in the hundreds of antique shops. The more expensive businesses are grouped around Faubourg Saint-Honoré, Faubourg Saint-Germain (rue de Seine, rue Jacob, rue des Saints-Pères, rue Bonaparte), in the Marais (village Saint-Paul) and the streets around the Pompidou Centre.

LE LOUVRE DES ANTIQUAIRES
Ⓜ *Palais-Royal*
2, place du Palais-Royal (1st)
Open daily except Monday
11 a.m.–7 p.m.
In a former department store, 250 up-market antique dealers.

VILLAGE SAINT-PAUL
Ⓜ *Saint-Paul*
Between quai des Célestins, rues Saint-Paul and Charlemagne (4th)
Open Thursday to Monday
11 a.m.– 7 p.m.
An enticing maze of streets where every other shop sells antiques.

LA COUR AUX ANTIQUAIRES
Ⓜ *Madeleine*
54, rue du Faubourg Saint-Honoré (8th)
Open daily 10.30 a.m.–6 p.m.; closed Monday morning.

Twenty dealers display their wares around a charming cobbled courtyard. Prices are high.

HÔTEL DROUOT
Ⓜ *Richelieu-Drouot*
9, rue Drouot (9th)
Prestigious auction rooms. For information, call 01 48 00 20 20, between 11 a.m. and 6 p.m.

VILLAGE SUISSE
Ⓜ *La Motte-Picquet-Grenelle*
78, ave de Suffren (15th)
Open Thursday to Monday,
10.30 a.m.–7 p.m.
The Swiss Pavilion, built for the 1889 World's Fair, has been taken over by a hundred dealers in antiques and curios.

❏ *BARGAINS*

ARMÉE DU SALUT
Ⓡ *Boulevard Masséna*
12, rue Cantagrel (13th)
Open Tuesday to Saturday
10 a.m.–noon and 2– 6 p.m.
Salvation Army warehouse. Who knows what you might find?

DÉPÔT-VENTE DE PARIS
Ⓜ *Porte de Vincennes*
81, rue de Lagny (20th)
Second-hand furniture in every style imaginable.

Eating Out

If you stayed in Paris long enough, you could eat your way not only round every French region, but also all the way around the world. The food scene is changing, becoming more international and more democratic. The number of fast-food outlets, self-services and sandwich bars is on the increase, much to the horror of gourmets and gastronomes but such a boon if you have to keep the children happy.

Don't fall into the trap of "tourist menus", generally chalked on blackboards displayed prominently on the café terraces: the French fries may be all right but you're bound to be disappointed by the steak. Our listing proposes a selection of restaurants, brasseries and bistros where you are sure to eat well at reasonable prices. Unless stated otherwise, they are open on Saturday and Sunday (but they often close for a month in July and August). Most places offer a fixed-price menu, service charge included (service compris).

❏ *RESTAURANTS*

AU PIED DE COCHON
Ⓜ *Louvre* or Ⓡ *Les Halles*
6, rue Coquillère (1st)
24-hour service.
If you fancy a grilled pig's trotter, some delicious seafood, or just a taste of the authentic Parisian atmosphere, this is the right place.

LE LOUCHÉBEM
Ⓜ *Châtelet*
31, rue Berger (1st)
Tel. 01 42 33 12 99.
Specializes in grilled meat. The chef was a butcher so knows what he's cooking.

L'INCROYABLE
Ⓜ *Palais-Royal–Musée du Louvre*
26, rue de Richelieu (1st)
Access also from 23, rue de Montpensier. Tel. 01 42 96 24 64. Closed Sunday and Monday.
A friendly little restaurant hidden down a narrow alley close to the Palais-Royal. The building dates from 1643. At lunchtime you can eat a three-course menu, wine included, for less than 100F. A few tables outside in summer. Unpretentious French food, such as *confit d'oie* with sauté potatoes, *andouillette* (tripe sausage), veal liver with blackcurrant sauce. Delicious *clafoutis* for dessert.

LE COCHON DORÉ
Ⓜ *Bonne-Nouvelle*
16, rue Thorel (2nd)
Tel. 01 42 33 29 70.
Specialities from Alsace *(quiche lorraine, choucroute)* in a rather rustic atmosphere.

LE GRAND COLBERT
Ⓜ *Richelieu-Drouot*
2, rue Vivienne (2nd)
Tel. 01 42 86 87 88.
Handsome brasserie in the Galerie Colbert; the fish soup and *bœuf gros sel* are highly acclaimed.

LE VAUDEVILLE
Ⓜ *Bourse*
29, rue Vivienne (2nd)
Tel. 01 40 20 04 62.
Classic brasserie fare in an Art Déco setting. Among the specialities: *choucroute*, fish and shellfish.

AMBASSADE D'AUVERGNE
Ⓜ *Rambuteau*
22, rue du Grenier-Saint-Lazare (3rd)
Tel. 01 42 72 31 22.
In a medieval building near the Pompidou Centre. Hearty Auvergnat dishes . Quite trendy, so book ahead.

AUBERGE NICOLAS FLAMEL
Ⓜ *Rambuteau*
51, rue Montmorency (3rd)
Tel. 01 42 71 77 78.
"Medieval" cuisine in one of the

oldest houses in Paris, the former home of a 15th-century alchemist.

BOFINGER

Ⓜ *Bastille*
5, rue de la Bastille (4th)
Tel. 01 42 72 87 82.
Traditional brasserie with glorious Belle Epoque décor. Book ahead.

LE VIEUX BISTRO

Ⓜ *Cité or Saint-Michel–Notre-Dame*
14, rue du Cloître-Notre-Dame (4th)
Tel. 01 43 54 18 95.
Popular bistro with a reputation for excellent French cuisine. Authentic décor.

MIRAVILE

Ⓜ *Pont-Marie*
72, quai de l'Hôtel de Ville (4th)
Tel. 01 42 74 72 22.
Gastronomic cuisine with the accent on originality. Very popular, book well ahead.

PERRAUDIN

ⓇⒺⓇ *Luxembourg*
157, rue Saint-Jacques (5th)
Tel. 01 46 33 15 75. Closed Saturday lunch, all Sunday, Monday lunch. No credit cards.
A friendly old bistrot in the heart of the student quarter, providing simple, home-style cooking for a young crowd.

LA TOUR D'ARGENT

Ⓜ *Maubert-Mutualité*
15–17, quai de la Tournelle (5th)
Tel. 01 43 54 23 51.
Closed Monday.
Highly reputed gastronomic restaurant with a superb view over the Seine. Rather pricey.

TASHI DELEK

ⓇⒺⓇ *Luxembourg*
4, rue des Fossés-St-Jacques (5th)
Tel. 01 43 26 55 55.
Closed Sunday.
This is the place to sample the taste of Tibet.

LA CLOSERIE DES LILAS

ⓇⒺⓇ *Port-Royal*
171, bd du Montparnasse (6th)
Tel. 01 40 51 34 50.
Open until 1.30 a.m.
Hemingway used to hang out here. Budding writers still do.

POLIDOR

Ⓜ *Odéon*
41, rue Monsieur-le-Prince (6th)
Tel. 01 43 26 95 34. No credit cards.
An old literary bistro; budget prices, excellent home-cooking and plenty of vintage charm.

CHEZ GERMAINE

Ⓜ *Vaneau*
30, rue Pierre-Leroux (7th)

*Tel. 01 42 73 28 34. Closed
Saturday evening, all Sunday, all
August.*
Very reasonable prices, relaxed
setting and hearty, if simple,
cuisine.

FOC LY
Ⓜ *La Motte-Piquet*
71, ave Suffren (7th)
Tel. 01 47 83 27 12.
Refined Chinese and Thai cuisine.
Book ahead.

LADURÉE
Ⓜ *Madeleine or Concorde*
16, rue Royale (8th)
Light cuisine in a beautiful, old-
fashioned décor.

LA FERMETTE MARBEUF 1900
Ⓜ *Alma-Marceau*
5, rue Marbeuf (8th)
Tel. 01 53 23 08 00.
Exquisite Art Nouveau setting
discovered only in 1978 when the
new owners decided to knock down
the walls. Classic cuisine.
Book 4–5 days ahead.

LE BŒUF SUR LE TOIT
Ⓜ *Saint-Philippe-du-Roule*
34, rue du Colisée (8th)
Tel. 01 43 59 83 80.
Very busy brasserie belonging to the
Flo chain. Magnificent 1930s décor,
attentive service.

L'ÉTOILE MAROCAINE
Ⓜ *Boissière*
56, rue Galilée (8th)
Tel. 01 47 20 54 45.
Tasty Moroccan specialities. Book
ahead.

VILLAGE D'UNG ET LI LAM
Ⓜ *Franklin-D.-Roosevelt*
10, rue Jean-Mermoz (8th)
Tel. 01 42 25 99 79.
Spicy Thai and Chinese cuisine.

CHARTIER
Ⓜ *Rue Montmartre*
7, rue du Faubourg Montmartre (9th)
Tel. 01 47 70 86 29.
A cheerful, noisy place with good,
basic food; menus around 80F. This
historic monument seats 1,300 but
you might have to queue.

FLO
Ⓜ *Château d'Eau*
7, cour des Petites-Écuries (10th)
Tel. 01 47 70 13 59.
Founded back in 1886 as a beer
warehouse, this was the first of the
Flo brasseries. Famous for shellfish.

JULIEN
Ⓜ *Strasbourg–Saint-Denis*
*16, rue du Faubourg
Saint-Denis (10th)*
Tel. 01 47 70 12 06.
Classic French cuisine in this superb
brasserie in authentic Art Nouveau

style, which started life as a
bouillon (a soup kitchen).

TERMINUS NORD
Ⓜ *Gare du Nord*
23, rue de Dunkerque (10th)
Tel. 01 42 85 05 15.
Handy for the railway station, good
shellfish and *choucroute*.

LE TRAIN BLEU
Ⓜ *Gare de Lyon*
Gare de Lyon (upstairs)
20, bd Diderot (12th)
Tel. 01 43 43 09 06.
Open daily until 11 p.m.
It's expensive, but worth every
centime if just for the palatial
setting. There's no other station
buffet like this one, a listed historic
monument. Cuisine "bourgeoise".
Book well ahead.

SAINTE-AMARANTE
Ⓜ *Bastille*
4, rue Biscornet (12th)
Tel. 01 43 43 00 08. Closed
Saturday, Sunday, Monday
evening and Tuesday evening.
French cuisine with the accent on
novelty; near Opéra Bastille.

LA CAGOUILLE
Ⓜ *Gaîté*
10 & 12, place C. Brancusi (14th)
Tel. 01 43 22 09 01.
Imaginative fish and shellfish dishes.

LE VIN DES RUES
Ⓜ *Denfert-Rochereau*
21, rue Boulard (14th)
Tel. 01 43 22 19 78.
Open Tuesday, Thursday,
Saturday 10 a.m.–8 p.m.;
Wednesday and Friday 9 p.m. to
midnight. No credit cards.
Regional dishes; try the excellent
pot au feu (beef and other meats
boiled with vegetables).

DATCHA LYDIE
Ⓜ *Dupleix*
7, rue Dupleix (15th)
Tel. 01 45 66 67 77.
Closed Wednesday.
Food with a Russian accent, in very
pleasant surroundings.

YVES QUINTARD
Ⓜ *Vaugirard*
99, rue Blomet (15th)
Tel. 01 42 50 22 27.
Closed Saturday lunchtime and all
day Sunday.
Innovative gourmet food. The
paintings on the walls are for sale.

LE COLONIAL
Ⓜ *Alma-Marceau*
Port Debilly,
Quai de New York (16th)
Tel. 01 53 23 98 98.
On a 70-m boat moored almost
opposite the Eiffel Tower, a smart
restaurant (spicy French cuisine),

with a bar in the first-class cabins and a nightclub (free admission) on the lower decks.

LE PETIT RÉTRO
Ⓜ Victor-Hugo
5, rue Mesnil (16th)
Tel. 01 44 05 06 05.
Closed Saturday lunch and Sunday.

Attractive little bistro, simple, homely cooking.

OH POIVRIER
Ⓜ Mirabeau
1, ave de Versailles (16th)
Tel. 01 42 88 20 22.

Chic bistro, relaxed atmosphere (several other branches throughout the city).

LES BOUCHONS DE FRANÇOIS CLERC
Ⓜ Villiers
22, rue de la Terrasse (17th)
Tel. 01 42 27 31 51. Closed Saturday and Sunday.

Dine to music at Les Bouchons… Classy food and classical recitals every evening. Fairly expensive.

LA BUTTE EN VIGNE
Ⓜ Abbesses
5, rue Poulbot (18th)
Tel. 01 46 06 91 96.

Traditional cuisine and lively music in a typical old Montmartre setting.

¡AY CARAMBA!
Ⓜ Botzaris
59, rue de Mouzaïa (19th)
Tel. 01 42 41 23 80.

Mexican food, mariachi music and crowded, party atmosphere.

❏ WINE BARS
The Parisian wine bar is something really special; the atmosphere is so very French. Everyone shouts and argues and gesticulates in typical Gallic fashion. And the food is good. There's usually a dish of the day, something homely and filling like lentils and salt pork. Or, for those who just want a snack, good pâtés, smoked ham and rillettes. Excellent wine sold by the glass.

LA TAVERNE HENRI IV
Ⓜ Pont-Neuf
13, place du Pont-Neuf (1st)
Tel. 01 43 54 27 90. Closed Saturday evening and Sunday.

WILLI'S WINE BAR
Ⓜ Bourse or Pyramides
13, rue des Petits-Champs (1st)
Tel. 01 42 61 05 09.
Closed Sunday.

LA TARTINE
Ⓜ St-Paul
24, rue de Rivoli (4th)
Tel. 01 42 72 76 85.

Closed Tuesdays and Wednesday mornings.

MA BOURGOGNE

Ⓜ *Saint-Paul*
19, place des Vosges (4th)
Tel. 01 42 78 44 64.

LE SAUVIGNON

Ⓜ *Sèvres-Babylone*
80, rue des Saints-Pères (7th)
Tel. 01 45 48 49 02.
Closed Sunday.

BISTROT DU SOMMELIER

Ⓜ *Saint-Augustin*
97, bd Haussmann (8th)
Tel. 01 42 65 24 85. Closed Saturday and Sunday.

LE PÈRE TRANQUILLE

Ⓜ *Montparnasse-Bienvenüe*
30, ave du Maine (15th)
Tel. 01 42 22 88 12.
Closed Sunday.

AU NÉGOCIANT

Ⓜ *Château-Rouge*
27, rue Lambert (18th)
Tel. 01 46 06 15 11. Closed Saturday and Sunday.

❏ *CAFÉS*

For a glimpse of real Parisian life, take your breakfast in a corner café: flaky croissants and coffee.

Cafés tend to open very early and close very late. All kinds of drinks are served, and snacks such as ham, cheese or salami sandwiches (made from a big chunk of crusty *baguette*), *croque-monsieur* (toasted ham-and-cheese sandwich, generally rather dry sliced bread), mixed salads and so on. Prices are variable, depending on whether you are sitting at the counter, at an inside table or outside on the terrace. If you ask for *"un café"*, you'll be served a small cup of strong black coffee; if you want milk in it, ask for *"un crème"*. Request *"une bière"*, and you'll get a bottled beer; for a glass of draught beer (half a litre), which you'll probably find a little pale, the term is *"un demi pression"*. Wine is served in a small glass called a *"ballon"*, so if you want red wine, ask for *"un ballon de rouge"*; white is *blanc*. The tip is always included *(service compris)*.

ANGELINA

Ⓜ *Tuileries*
226, rue de Rivoli (1st)
Tel. 01 42 60 82 00.
Open 9 a.m.–7 p.m.
There's a hushed atmosphere in this restaurant and tea room opposite the Tuileries. The hot chocolate and Mont Blanc dessert (chestnut purée, whipped cream and a nugget of meringue) are simply *exquis*.

CAFÉ MARLY
Ⓜ Palais-Royal
Palais du Louvre, Cour Napoléon (1st)
Tel. 01 49 26 06 60.
Open until 2 a.m.
Smart café overlooking the famous pyramid.

CAFÉ BEAUBOURG
Ⓜ Rambuteau
100, rue Saint-Martin (4th)
Tel. 01 48 87 63 96.
Open until 2 a.m.
Opposite the Pompidou Centre, airy, stylish and modern.

CAFÉ DE FLORE
Ⓜ Saint-Germain-des-Prés
172, bd Saint-Germain (6th)
Tel. 01 45 48 55 26.
Open until 1.30 a.m.
It became famous in the days of Existentialism, when Simone de Beauvoir and Jean-Paul Sartre came here to keep warm. Still today, you can eavesdrop on the intellectuals trying to put the world to rights.

LE PROCOPE
Ⓜ Odéon
13, rue de l'Ancienne-Comédie (6th)
Tel. 01 40 46 79 00.
Open until 1 a.m.
Very old café (founded 1686), once patronized by great writers and politicians such as Diderot, Danton, Marat, Rousseau and Voltaire.

LES DEUX MAGOTS
Ⓜ Saint-Germain-des-Prés
6, place Saint-Germain-des-Prés (6th)
Tel. 01 45 48 55 25.
Open 7.30 a.m.–1.30 a.m.
Writers Camus, Jacques Prévert and Sartre scribbled their first lines within these walls. The terrace tables, if you can grab an empty seat, are simply great for people-watching.

LE FOUQUET'S
Ⓜ George V
99, ave des Champs-Elysées (8th)
Tel. 01 47 23 70 60.
Open until 1 a.m.
A Champs-Elysées institution. Everyone that's anyone comes to Fouquet's (like the French football team after a match), and unless you have a famous face it isn't easy to get past the door.

LA COUPOLE
Ⓜ Vavin
102, bd du Montparnasse (14th)
Tel. 01 43 20 14 20.
Open until 2 a.m.
The rendez-vous of artists and intellectuals ever since it was opened in 1927.
Local artists were commissioned for the paintings on the pillars, their salary amounting to credit for unlimited drinks.

Entertainment

The best way of finding out what's on is to invest three francs in the Pariscope or l'Officiel des Spectacles, weekly listings magazines with information on all the films, concerts, operas, plays, variety shows that liven up Parisian nights. Pariscope has an English supplement edited by Time Out, with reviews and an up-to-date rundown of the club scene. See page 46 for how to book seats.

❏ *NATIONAL THEATRES*

COMÉDIE FRANÇAISE
Ⓜ *Palais-Royal*
2, rue de Richelieu (1st)
Tel. 01 44 58 15 15.
A wide range of classics from Molière through Racine to Feydeau,

played by first-class actors. Recently refurbished.

OPÉRA COMIQUE
Ⓜ *Richelieu-Drouot*
5, rue Favart (2nd)
Tel. 01 42 44 45 46.
Opera and operetta.

HOW TO BOOK

Tickets are usually put on sale two weeks before opening night. You can book seats through your travel agents, through your hotel concierge, at Virgin Megastore, 52, avenue des Champs-Elysées, at the FNAC store at Forum des Halles (level –3), or at the venues themselves. Half-price theatre tickets for performances the same day are sold at Kiosque Théâtre, Place de la Madeleine (open Tuesday to Saturday 12.30–8 p.m.). Special discounts are usually available for children, students (international student's card required), and the over 60s.

OPÉRA GARNIER

Ⓜ *Opéra*
Place de l'Opéra (2nd)
Tel. 01 44 73 13 00.
Ballet, classic and modern in the splendidly renovated opera house.

ODÉON THÉÂTRE DE L'EUROPE

Ⓜ *Odéon* or Ⓡ *Luxembourg*
1, place Paul Claudel (6th)
Tel. 01 44 41 36 36.
Hosts theatrical troupes from all over Europe, performing in their native language.

THÉÂTRE DU VIEUX COLOMBIER

Ⓜ *Saint Sulpice*
21, rue du Vieux-Colombier (6th)
Tel. 01 44 39 87 00.

Comédie Française actors perform a classical and modern repertoire.

OPÉRA BASTILLE

Ⓜ *Bastille*
Place de la Bastille (11th)
Tel. 01 44 73 13 00.
Opera, operetta, concerts, ballet, plays and cabaret.

THÉÂTRE NATIONAL DE CHAILLOT

Ⓜ *Trocadéro*
Place du Trocadéro (16th)
Tel. 01 47 27 81 15.
Mainly classical drama.

THÉÂTRE NATIONAL DE LA COLLINE

Ⓜ *Gambetta*
15, rue Malte-Brun (20th)
Tel. 01 44 62 52 52.
Two theatres showing works by young, contemporary playwrights.

❏ CLUBLAND

You may find it difficult to get into the trendiest places without a membership card, but you can always try your luck by arriving unfashionably early. Things don't usually get started until at least midnight. Some clubs charge an entry fee that includes the first drink *(consommation)*, while others offer free entry and charge the earth for drinks.

REX CLUB
Ⓜ *Bonne Nouvelle*
5, bd Poissonnière (2nd)
Tel. 01 42 36 83 98.
Techno, grunge, heavy metal: a
different trend every night.

LES BAINS
Ⓜ *Etienne-Marcel*
7, rue du Bourg-l'Abbé (3rd)
Tel. 01 48 87 01 80.
Willowy models, top designers and
fashion victims flock to this old
white-tiled public bathhouse.

LE SAINT
Ⓜ *Saint-Michel*
7, rue Saint-Séverin (5th)
Tel. 01 43 25 50 04.
All the latest hits in this very
popular club.

ZED CLUB
Ⓜ *Maubert-Mutualité*
2, rue des Anglais (5th)
Tel. 01 43 54 93 78.
You'll love this place if you feel
nostalgic for the rock'n'roll era.
Closed Sunday to Tuesday.

CASTEL
Ⓜ *Mabillon*
15, rue Princesse (6th)
Tel. 01 40 51 52 80.
One of the oldest nightclubs
(private) that somehow rides
smoothly over the latest trends.

THE VILLAGE
Ⓜ *Pigalle*
40, rue Fontaine (9th)
Tel. 01 40 16 40 24.
Friday and Saturday from midnight,
disco hits of the 70s and 80s.

LA JAVA
Ⓜ *Belleville*
*105, rue du Faubourg du
Temple (10th)*
Tel. 01 42 02 20 52.
Live bands bring Latin sounds to this
venerable nightclub where Edith Piaf
and Maurice Chevalier used to
tango the night away.

LE BATACLAN
Ⓜ *Bastille*
50, bd Voltaire (11th)
Tel. 01 47 00 30 12.
Old-time dance hall with disco and
funk at weekends.

LA CASBAH
Ⓜ *Ledru-Rollin*
18, rue Forge-Royale (11th)
Tel. 01 43 71 71 89.
An "Arabian Nights" décor for an
easy-going gathering.

LA CHAPELLE DES LOMBARDS
Ⓜ *Bastille*
19, rue de Lappe (11th)
Tel. 01 43 57 24 24.
All kinds of music, from afro-rock to
zouk. Closed Sunday and Monday.

❏ *JAZZ CLUBS, BARS AND PIANO BARS*

BAISER SALÉ
Ⓜ *Châtelet*
58, rue des Lombards (1st)
Tel. 01 42 33 37 71.
Live jazz and blues.

PETIT OPPORTUN
Ⓜ *Châtelet*
15, rue des Lavandières-Sainte-Opportune (1st)
Tel. 01 42 36 01 36.
Live concerts from 11 p.m.

HARRY'S NEW YORK BAR
Ⓜ *Opéra*
5, rue Daunou (2nd)
Tel. 01 42 61 71 14.
Intimate atmosphere and cool music.

KITTY O'SHEA'S PUB
Ⓜ *Opéra*
10, rue des Capucines (2nd)
Tel. 01 40 15 00 30.
Duplicate of the famous Dublin pub.

CAVEAU DE LA HUCHETTE
Ⓜ *Saint-Michel*
5, rue de la Huchette (5th)
Tel. 01 43 26 65 05.
Trad jazz in a smoky, crowded cellar, from 9.30 every evening.

PETIT JOURNAL SAINT-MICHEL
Ⓡ *Luxembourg*
71, bd Saint-Michel (5th)
Tel. 01 43 26 28 59.
Congenial atmosphere, New Orleans jazz. Closed Sunday.

ALLIANCE SAINT-GERMAIN-DES-PRÉS
Ⓜ *Saint-Germain-des-Prés*
7–11, rue Saint-Benoît (6th)
Tel. 01 42 61 53 53.
Jazz concerts until 2 a.m.

LE BILBOQUET
Ⓜ *Saint-Germain-des-Prés*
13, rue Saint-Benoît (6th)
Tel. 01 45 48 81 84.
Dine to music in Saint-Germain.

LE MONTANA
Ⓜ *Saint-Germain-des-Prés*
28, rue Saint-Benoît (6th)
Tel. 01 42 22 77 00.
Jazz club in the basement, bar upstairs. Open from 10.30 p.m.

LE LUTÈCE
Ⓜ *Sèvres-Babylone*
Hôtel Lutétia
45, bd Raspail (6th)
Tel. 01 49 54 46 46.
Live jazz Thursday, Friday and Saturday from 9 p.m. to 1 a.m.

NEW MORNING
Ⓜ *Château d'Eau*
7–9, rue des Petites Ecuries (10th)
Tel. 01 45 23 56 39.

Concerts from 8.30 p.m., with some of the best jazz and blues performers.

MÉRIDIEN
Ⓜ *Porte Maillot*
81, bd Gouvion Saint-Cyr (17th)
Tel. 01 40 68 30 42.
Jazz Club Lionel Hampton, top-of-the-bill performers from 10.30 p.m. till 2 a.m.

❏ CABARET AND CAFÉ-THÉÂTRE

CAVEAU DE LA RÉPUBLIQUE
Ⓜ *République*
1, bd Saint-Martin (3rd)
Tel. 01 42 78 44 45.
For those with brilliant French: chansonniers and political satire.

CAFÉ DE LA GARE
Ⓜ *Hôtel de Ville*
41, rue du Temple (4th)
Tel. 01 42 78 52 51.
Café-théâtre is the French equivalent of "alternative" comedy. This is one of the best.

PARADIS LATIN
Ⓜ *Cardinal Lemoine*
28, rue du Cardinal-Lemoine (5th)
Tel. 01 43 25 28 28. Book ahead.
Dinner, smooth orchestra and girlie revue.

CRAZY HORSE SALOON
Ⓜ *George V*
12, ave George-V (8th)
Tel. 01 47 23 32 32.
Variety show with gorgeous girls.

LIDO
Ⓜ *George V*
116bis, ave des Champs-Elysées (8th)
Tel. 01 40 76 56 10. Book ahead.
Dinner-dance and revue with the famous Bluebell Girls.

FOLIES BERGÈRE
Ⓜ *Cadet or Rue Montmartre*
32, rue Richer (9th)
Tel. 01 44 79 98 98.
Closed Monday.
Dinner at 7 p.m., famous "follies" start at 9 p.m.

BAL DU MOULIN ROUGE
Ⓜ *Blanche*
82, bd de Clichy (18th)
Tel. 01 46 06 00 19. Book ahead.
Dinner dance and glamorous girls. Shows at 9 and 11 p.m.

CHEZ MICHOU
Ⓜ *Pigalle*
80, rue des Martyrs (18th)
Tel. 01 46 06 16 04. No credit cards.
Hilarious drag show starts at 11 p.m. Dinner (reservation only) 8.30 p.m.

Excursions

Why confine yourself to the big city sights, when there's so much to see in the outskirts? These are popular day trips from Paris, most of them easily reached by RER train.

CHÂTEAUX DE MALMAISON AND BOIS-PRÉAU

1, ave du Château,
92500 Rueil-Malmaison
Ⓡ *line A1 to Rueil-Malmaison,*
then bus 258A to château.
Open daily (except Tuesday)
10 a.m.–noon and 1.30–5 p.m.

Empress Josephine, wife of Napoleon Bonaparte, bought the château at Malmaison in 1799 and lived there, devoting most of her time to gardening, until she died of a chill in 1814. The rooms, all charming, are full of souvenirs of Napoleon's boyhood and Josephine's personal belongings. The neighbouring château of Bois-Préau has been turned into a museum (access with the same ticket) documenting Napoleon's exile on the island of St Helena.

DISNEYLAND PARIS

Disneyland Theme Park,
77777 Marne-la-Vallée
Ⓡ *line A4 direction Marne-la-*
Vallée/Chessy; station: Chessy.
Trains every 20 minutes; the last
train for Paris (direction Saint-
Germain-en-Laye) leaves at 20
past midnight.
Open all year, 10 a.m.–6 p.m.
(longer in summer).

Don your best Mickey Mouse ears and spend a day or two "chez Mickey" as the Parisians call this chunk of American culture that has firmly taken root in Marne-la-Vallée. Five "lands": Main Street, U.S.A., Frontierland, Adventureland, Fantasyland and Discoveryland. Hotel complex, golf course, campsite and Disney Village (shops, bars and restaurants), not to mention all the thrills and spills of Buffalo Bill's Wild West Show.

MUSÉE DE L'AIR ET DE L'ESPACE

Le Bourget Airport
Bus: line 350 from gare du Nord
or Ⓡ line B then bus 152
Open daily (except Monday)
10 a.m.–5 p.m. (until 6 p.m. from
May to October).

From Clément Ader's first plane (1897) to *fusée Ariane,* two hundred magnificent flying machines recount the history of aviation and the conquest of space.

PARC ASTÉRIX

60128 Plailly
Ⓡ *line B3 – Roissy-Charles-de-*
Gaulle, then shuttle bus, every
half hour from 9.30 a.m. to
1.30 p.m., return from 4–8 p.m.
Open 10 a.m.–6 p.m. April to
October, until 7 p.m. on June
weekends and every day in July
and August. For information,
tel. 03 44 62 34 34.

In their village in the Gaul's Forest, France's immortal comic-strip heroes Asterix, Obelix and the druid Getafix are still holding out against Roman attack, with a little help from the druid's magic potion. Theme park with shows, shops, restaurants, performing dolphins and seals. Picnicking allowed.

CHÂTEAU DE VERSAILLES

78000 Versailles
Ⓜ *Pont de Sèvres + bus 171*
or Ⓡ line C – Versailles RG
Open daily (except Monday)
9 a.m.–6 p.m. in summer (until
5.30 p.m. in winter).
Grand Trianon and Petit Trianon
open daily in summer 11 a.m.–
6.30 p.m. (in winter, Tuesday to
Friday 10 a.m.–12.30 p.m. and
2–5.30 p.m.; Saturday and Sunday
10 a.m.–5.30 p.m.)

Take a full day to visit the extravagant home of the kings of France, from Louis XIV (1678) to

Louis XVI (1789). With all their gilt, marble, crystal, paintings and tapestries, the grand apartments are overwhelming, perfectly matching the vainglorious character of the Sun King, Louis XIV. The formal gardens, studded with statues, cooled by ponds and fountains, are a delight. The fountains play to music on Sunday afternoons in summer. Walk to the more modest Grand and Petit Trianon palaces, and Marie-Antoinette's "hamlet" in the woods, where the Queen fancied she was "returning to nature".

FRANCE MINIATURE

25, ave du Mesnil,
78990 Elancourt
Ⓡ line C7 – Saint-Quentin-en-Yvelines or train: Gare Montparnasse to Saint-Quentin then shuttle bus.
Open March to mid-November, daily 10 a.m.–7 p.m.

All the historic monuments of France and 15 typical villages, scaled down to a 30th of their real size, on this 9-acre 3-dimensional map.

GIVERNY: CLAUDE MONET'S HOUSE

27620 Giverny
Train: Gare Saint-Lazare. Take the Rouen train as far as Vernon, then bus or taxi to Giverny. You can hire a bicycle at Vernon station

UNDERGROUND ENTERTAINMENT

The Paris métro is a hotbed of talent. The endless corridors echo with a Bach partita played by a first-class conservatory student, or the flamenco efforts of a passionate guitarist. Even classical cellists lug their instruments down under. They're in it for the money, and to keep warm in winter.

Buskers of all levels of expertise also travel the trains. The classics give way to traditional accordionists, singers of dubious talent accompanied by ghetto blasters, marimba players, even puppeteers who erect a stage at the end of the carriage. It's all part of the local colour, and it can't cost you more than a coin.

(7 km, 4 miles from Giverny).
Open April to October, daily except Monday, 10 a.m.–6 p.m.

You won't see any originals in the house and studio of Claude Monet, only photographic reproductions of his paintings. But no one is disappointed by the Japanese water garden complete with weeping willows, wooden bridges, and the waterlilies that inspired so many of the artist's works.

CHÂTEAU DE CHANTILLY

60631 Chantilly
Ⓡ *line D Chantilly*
*Open June to August 9.30 a.m.–
5 or 6 p.m. (winter 9.30 a.m.–
12.30 p.m. and 2–5 p.m.). Closed
Tuesdays and public holidays.*

The castle of Chantilly, surrounded by a peaceful park, houses the Condé Museum, a prestigious collection of Old Masters such as Raphael, Poussin and Watteau. In the library, admire the famous illuminated Book of Hours, *Les Très Riches Heures du Duc de Berry*, illustrating medieval life. Equestrian shows are presented in the 18th-century Great Stables, opposite the castle, in the Living Horse Museum *(Musée Vivant du Cheval)*. Opening times differ from above, with special hours for dressage demonstrations; for information tel. 01 44 57 13 13.

CHÂTEAU DE FONTAINEBLEAU

77300 Fontainebleau
*Train: Gare de Lyon, then bus.
Open daily except Tuesday and
public holidays 9.30 a.m.–
12.30 p.m. and 2–5 p.m.*

The kings of France came to Fontainebleau to hunt in the great forest. François I built the palace in 1527, and it became the artistic centre of the French Renaissance. Museum devoted to Napoleon I and his family in the Louis XV wing, and a Chinese Museum created by Empress Eugénie.

VAUX LE VICOMTE

77950 Maincy
Ⓡ *line D to Melun, then taxi
(7 km).
Open in summer 10 a.m.– 6 p.m.
(winter 11 a.m.– 5 p.m.)*

Louis XIV had a fit when he saw this splendid château that his Finance Minister Nicolas Fouquet had built for himself. Fouquet was jailed, and the king commissioned the Vaux le Vicomte architects Le Vau, Le Brun and Le Nôtre to build Versailles. The fountains play on Saturday evenings in summer. Guided tours of the château by candlelight, every Saturday evening from 6.30 to 11 p.m., May to September.

FUTUROSCOPE

86130 Jaunay-Clan
*Train: TGV from Gare de
Montparnasse, 90 min.
Open daily 9 a.m.–dusk; late
closing (nocturne) and laser show
all July and August, weekends
and public holidays from end
March to mid-November.*

Near Poitiers, the European Park of the Moving Image presents visual fantasies on giant, circular and multiple screens in a setting of out-of-this-world architecture.

The Hard Facts

Babysitting
For some time out on the town without the children, put them in the care of Ababa, Une Maman en Plus, tel. 01 45 49 46 46; or Kid Service, tel. 01 47 66 00 52.

Climate
Paris enjoys a mild continental climate, with average daily temperatures of 15–19°C (59–66°F) in summer and 3–7°C (37–45°F) in winter. The weather is changeable, so it's advisable to have a folding umbrella handy—particularly in winter, when it can be even rainier in Paris than in London. July and August are often stiflingly hot.

Customs and entry formalities
Nationals of the U.S., Canada, Switzerland and EU countries require a passport or National Identity Card to enter France. No visa is required. Nationals from Australia and South Africa require passport *and* visa.

In principle, travel between France and other parties to the Schengen agreement of 1995 (Belgium, Germany, Luxembourg, Netherlands, Portugal and Spain) will be without documentation check at immigration controls. However, it may be some time until implementation takes effect everywhere.

French Customs authorizes the duty-free importation (for those over 17 years of age) of 200 cigarettes, 50 cigars or 250 g tobacco, and 1 litre spirits and 2 litres wine; for those arriving from EU countries with goods on which the duty has already been paid, the allowance increases to 800 cigarettes or 200 cigars or 1 kg tobacco, and 10 litres spirits and 90 litres wine.

Articles purchased in France are subject to VAT, or value-added tax. If you have spent at least 2,000F in any one shop, reside outside the EU, and are leaving France for a non-EU country, you may reclaim this tax (about a 13 per cent return after administration fees). Ask the shopkeeper for the necessary *détaxe* papers.

Disabled
The major Parisian museums will provide a wheelchair if you ring in advance with your request. Many have an escort service as well. At the Louvre, there's a special lift for the dis-

abled under the glass pyramid—avoiding the escalator—to the reception hall, where they pick up their wheelchair. In the older galleries, guards will even open up doors closed to the general public to provide easier wheelchair access. The Louvre will suggest special tours planned for good mobility.

The Paris Tourist Office can provide you with a brochure entitled *Paris: Musées et Monuments*, in which the places are coded with symbols indicating wheelchair access, hire and escort service.

Paris's métros and buses are unsuitable for wheelchairs, but RER lines A and B are accessible in part. The RATP transport network has a *voyage accompagné* service, in which the disabled are accompanied by someone during their voyage. Available from 9 a.m. to 5 p.m.; tel. 01 49 59 96 00 at least 48 hours in advance. The English-language book *Access in Paris* is available from W. H. Smith, 248, rue de Rivoli.

Driving

The speed limit is 50 kph (30 mph) in town, 80 kph (50 mph) on ring roads, and 130 kph (80 mph) on motorways. France drives on the right and requires seat belts to be worn in both front and rear seats. Children under 10 may not sit in the front seat. Horns should not be sounded in town. Do not drive in bus lanes even in a traffic jam.

In most of Paris, parking places have meters, with hourly tariffs ranging between 5 and 10F per hour and a maximum stay of 2 hours. Car parks cost between 5 and 75F per hour.

Breakdown service is available from SOS Dépannage, tel. 01 47 07 99 99. For driving information, call the Centre Régional d'Informations Routières on 01 48 99 33 33.

Electrical current

220-volt, 50 cycles AC. Plugs have two round prongs, so you will require adaptors if travelling with electrical appliances.

Emergencies

In a real emergency, dial **17** for the police or **18** for the fire brigade *(pompiers)*. Other useful numbers:

SAMU, 24-hour ambulance: tel. **15**.

SOS Médecins, for 24-hour house calls: tel. 01 47 07 77 77.

SOS Dentaire, dental emergencies: tel. 01 43 37 51 00.

SOS Cardiologues, cardiological emergencies: tel. 01 47 07 50 50.

Anti-poison centre, tel. 01 40 37 04 04.

Pharmacie Dhéry, 84, ave des Champs-Elysées (8th), métro George V, tel. 01 45 62 02 41, is open day and night.

American Hospital, 63, bd Victor Hugo, 92202 Neuilly, métro Porte Maillot and bus 82, tel. 01 46 41 25 25.

Franco-British Hospital, 3, rue Barbès, 92300 Levallois-Perret, métro Anatole France, tel. 01 46 39 22 22.

British nationals are entitled to use the medical services of the French social security system but should obtain an E111 form at a U.K. post office before leaving home. Non-EU citizens are advised to take out health insurance before their trip.

Language

Don't worry if your French is not up to scratch, for the personnel in most hotels and restaurants will understand your English. France is coping bravely with the indignity of its tongue being superseded by English as the worldwide *lingua franca*. If you do give French a try, stick to *vous*, rather than the familiar *tu*, and remember that any lady over 30 should be addressed as *Madame*, not *Mademoiselle*.

Some everyday phrases and a little insight into the French way of life are included in *The French Way* section of this guide.

Lost and found

If you discover you have lost or been robbed of something, head to the nearest police station and make a declaration. Retain the receipt which you will be given for possible insurance claims. For objects lost in the métro or bus, inquire immediately at the terminus. If the object hasn't been found, inquire at the Bureau des objets trouvés, 36, rue des Morillons (15th). Open daily from 8.30 a.m., closing Monday Wednesday and Friday at 5 p.m., Tuesday and Thursday 8 p.m.

No information will be given over the telephone; you must visit the office or write, giving the date, place and time of loss and a description of the object.

Money matters

Banks generally open 9 a.m.–4.30 p.m., Monday to Friday. Bureaux de change usually keep later hours and open Saturday and Sunday as well. Chequepoint operates a 24-hour change at 150, avenue des Champs-Elysées.

Currency. The *franc* (F, FF, or Fr.) is divided into 100 *centimes* (ct.). Coins range from 5 ct. to 20 F; notes from 20 to 500 F.

Credit cards are usually accepted, but there may be a minimum limit of 100 F, and smaller restaurants and hotels frequently insist on cash, so it is wise to inquire ahead. If you want to use your card to withdraw francs from Paris's cashpoint machines, check with your bank that it is valid abroad and be sure to know your PIN number.

Traveller's cheques are widely accepted in Paris. Don't forget that you need your passport to cash them.

Eurocheques are only reluctantly accepted, as bank charges are high. You may need to pay a supplement to use this method of settling bills.

Post offices

Opening hours: 8 a.m.–7 p.m., Monday to Friday; 8 a.m.–noon on Saturday. Closed Sunday and holidays. The Central Post Office, 52, rue du Louvre (1st), is open 24 hours a day for all services, including fax (also on Sundays and holidays).

Public holidays

Banks and post offices are closed on:

January 1	New Year's Day
May 1	Labour Day
May 8	Victory Day, 1945)
July 14	Bastille Day
August 15	Assumption
November 1	All Saints' Day
November 11	Armistice Day, 1918)
December 25	Christmas Day
Movable dates:	Easter Monday Ascension Day Whit Monday

Safety precautions

It's sensible in a large city like Paris to keep valuable objects, large amounts of money, your passport and plane or train ticket in your hotel safe and to carry around only a little cash and a credit card. Travelling on the métro or on a bus late at night isn't advisable. Beware of pickpockets in the métro. Never carry your money in a rucksack, easy prey for thieves. If you park your car, remove the radio-cassette-CD player; never leave anything tempting in view.

Telephone

You can place local or international calls from any public telephone booth (instructions are given in English as well as French), of which there are two kinds: those that require coins—still found in cafés—and those that function with a phone card, or *télécarte*. The cards come in 50 or 120 units and are on sale in post offices, principal métro and RER stations, SNCF (train) ticket counters, France Télécom agencies, and tobacconists. Calls are cheaper after 7.30 p.m. and on weekends.

All French telephone numbers, with the exception of services, consist of 10 digits. To call anywhere in Paris or the rest of France, you have to dial the full 10-digit number.

To make an international call from Paris, dial 00, the country code (1 for USA and Canada, 44 for UK) then the area code (without the initial 0), and the local number. To enquire about other country codes, dial 12.

To call France from another country, dial 00 (or other applicable digits to reach an international line), then 33 (the country code for France) then the 10-digit number minus the initial zero.

Time

Paris is GMT + 1. Hence 5 p.m. in Paris is 4 p.m. in London and 11 a.m. in New York. Summer hours (GMT + 2) run from late March to end September.

French time is based on the 24-hour system; that is, midnight to noon is written as 0 to 12 *heures*, and noon to midnight as 12 to 24 *heures*. 14 h 30, for example, means 2.30 p.m.

Tipping

Restaurants automatically take care of the service charge, either by including it in the menu prices (*service compris*) or by adding an extra charge of 10 to 15 per cent to your bill. Taxi drivers should receive 10 per cent of the fare, a lavatory attendant expects a small tip (usually there's a conspicuous saucer), and a hotel porter should be tipped at least 5 F per bag.

Toilets

Scattered throughout Paris are coin-operated cubicles called Sanisettes (you need a 2-F coin). Failing these, use the facilities of a café—but order at least a coffee—or one of the big hotels or department stores. Toilets may be marked *Femmes* or *Dames* for women; *Hommes* or *Messieurs* for men; or simply *Toilettes* or *WC*.

Tourist information offices

The main office is at 127, avenue des Champs-Elysées, at the top on your left as you face the Arc de Triomphe. Métro Charles de Gaulle-Etoile or George V, tel. 01 49 52 53 54. The office is open daily (except May 1) from 9 a.m. to 8 p.m. and provides a wealth of information, guidebooks, posters, souvenirs, maps, foreign exchange, museum and RATP passes, excursion tickets. Other branches at the railway stations, the Eiffel Tower and the Mairie de Paris (29, rue de Rivoli).

Tours

Boat tours. Cruises with commentary along the Seine and the canals, lunch/tea/dinner cruises:

Bateaux-Mouches
Ⓜ Alma-Marceau,
tel. 01 42 25 96 10

Bateaux Parisiens
Ⓜ Bir-Hakeim/Iéna
tel. 01 44 11 33 44

Bateaux Vedettes de Paris
Ⓜ Bir Hakeim
tel. 01 47 05 71 29

Canauxrama
Ⓜ Jean-Jaurès
tel. 01 42 39 15 00

Les Vedettes du Pont-Neuf
Ⓜ Pont-Neuf
tel. 01 46 33 98 38

Paris Canal
Ⓜ Jean-Jaurès
tel. 01 42 40 96 97.

Bus tours. The *Balabus* circulates between the main tourist sites every Sunday and public holiday from spring through summer, 12.30–8 p.m. A complete round trip takes 50 min. Board at any stop marked "Balabus": Gare de Lyon, Saint-Michel, Musée d'Orsay, Louvre, Concorde, Champs-Elysées, etc.

The *Montmartrobus* makes a tour of the Montmartre hill. Terminus in Place Pigalle and town hall *(mairie)* of the 18th arrondissement.

Private sightseeing companies run 2-hour tours with commentaries in many languages:

Cityrama
tel. 01 44 55 61 00

Paris-Vision
tel. 01 42 60 30 01

Parisbus/Les Cars Rouges, tel. 01 42 30 55 50, is a hop-on/hop off service: you can get off at any stop and reboard the bus later. Tickets are valid two days and may be bought on the bus.

Walking tours. The English supplement in *Pariscope* lists details of guided walks in English. If you want to join a tour in French, look under the heading Conférences in *Pariscope* or the daily newspaper listings.

For a self-guided look at Paris, the "Planted Promenade" walkway runs 4.5 km (3 miles) east to west (about a third of it elevated above the traffic), from Place de la Bastille to the Bois de Vincennes. It is dotted with five gardens, and there are lanes for pedestrians and cyclists. Other itineraries available at the tourist office.

From the Austerlitz bridge to the Invalides bridge, a 5-km (3-mile) path along the quays is reserved for pedestrians only.

The particularly scenic stretch of embankment between the Sully and Iéna bridges has been designated by UNESCO as a World Heritage site.

Transport

Métro. Wherever you are, wherever you go, there is always a métro station nearby to provide efficient underground transport. Locate your destination on a métro map and follow the various lines by their colour, number and, to ensure that you find the right platform *(quai)*, the name of the terminus corresponding to the direction you're headed. This terminus is signposted on the platform and in all the access corridors. The itinerary of the line is displayed in the interior of the métro car.

You need to transfer to another line? This can involve a long walk through a maze of corridors. On the platform, follow the orange "Correspondance" signs to your new direction.

Near the station exit *(Sortie)*, consult the map of the immediate neighbourhood and you'll find the way to your final destination in a snap. Exits are usually indicated for even *(pairs)* and odd *(impairs)* street numbers.

First departures from the terminus stations are at 5.30 a.m.; last arrivals at 1.15 a.m.

RER. This ultra-rapid transportation system links Paris with the suburbs. You can switch easily from the métro to the RER, as the two networks are interconnected. Be sure to keep your ticket handy; you will need it when you leave the system and for spot-checks. An RER ticket from the suburbs to Paris is also valid on the metro.

The first trains leave the terminus stations at 5.30 a.m.; last departures, 00.30 a.m.

Bus. Getting around by bus is a good way to see the city. The explanatory information posted at the bus stops will guide you. As long as you stay on the same line, you will need only one ticket.

The timetable varies according to the line; on Sundays and holidays, as well as evenings after 8.30 p.m., the service is less frequent. If you wish a bus to stop so you can board, raise your hand as a signal; inside, ring the buzzer to get off. RATP information: tel. 01 43 46 14 14.

The *Noctambus*, or night bus, travels 10 routes. Buses leave from Châtelet every hour between 1.30 and 5.30 a.m. and fan out to the city limits.

The principal tourist neighbourhoods are served by the following bus lines:

Line 21
Gare Saint-Lazare – Auber –
Avenue de l'Opéra – Palais
Royal – Rue de Rivoli –
Boulevard Saint-Michel –
Luxembourg – Rue Gay-Lussac
– Cité universitaire – Porte de
Gentilly.

Line 30
Gare de l'Est – Anvers –
Place Pigalle – Place de Clichy
– Place des Ternes – Place
Charles-de-Gaulle-Etoile –
Trocadéro.

Line 54
Porte de Clichy – Place de
Clichy – Place Pigalle –
Anvers – Gare du Nord – Gare
de l'Est – République.

Line 67
Place Pigalle – Richelieu-
Drouot – Louvre – Place du
Châtelet – Hôtel de Ville –
Jardin des Plantes – Porte de
Gentilly.

Line 74
Porte de Clichy – Place de
Clichy – Place Saint-Georges –
Louvre – Place du Châtelet –
Hôtel de Ville.

Line 81
Porte Saint-Ouen – Place de
Clichy – Rue d'Amsterdam –
Opéra – Louvre – Place du
Châtelet.

Line 95
Porte Montmartre – Place de
Clichy – Gare Saint-Lazare –
Opéra – Louvre – Saint-
Germain-des-Prés – Gare
Montparnasse.

Tickets. Tickets for métro and
bus are on sale singly (8F) or in
booklets *(carnet)* of 10 (46F).
One ticket suffices for a journey
by métro or RER within Paris on
any number of lines; one ticket is
required for the bus as long as
you stay on the same line.

It's worth buying one of the
following passes if you intend to
use public transport

Mobilis. Valid for one day,
without restriction, on the bus
network, métro, RER, suburban
SNCF trains, Montmartre funicular. Available for 2 to 8 zones.
Zone 5 covers Versailles, Orly
and Roissy airports and Chessy
(the stop for Disneyland Paris).
Prices from 30F to 110F.

Paris-Visite Card. Valid for
1 to 5 days over the entire network of the RATP, RER, SNCF
Paris and Ile-de-Paris, with an
option of 3, 5 or 8 zones. The
pass also offers discounts at
several tourist sites (museums,
boat excursions, shops, amuse-
ments). (A 2-day pass is sold to
tour operators; it is not available
to the general public.) Prices
from 50F to 350F.

Carte Orange. Available for one week or one month for 2 to 8 zones. Requires photo. Valid for same means of transport as *Paris-Visite* with the exception of Orlyval. 1996 prices: weekly pass, from 63F for 2 zones to 189F for 8 zones; monthly pass, from 219F for 2 zones to 660F for 8 zones.

For access to the métro or RER platforms, slide your pass into the turnstile slot. You need to do the same thing at the exit.

In the bus, show your card to the conductor without punching it in the validating machine.

Batobus. Regularly scheduled boats make 5 stops along the Seine, from the Eiffel Tower to Notre-Dame, from 10 a.m. to 7.30 p.m., April to September. 1996 prices: 12F from one stop to the next; day pass 60F.

To and from the airport
From Roissy-Charles-de-Gaulle, *Roissy Rail* (RER line B) takes 35 minutes to reach central Paris, where you can transfer to the métro. Departures every 15 min.

Air France buses take 40 min., with departures every 15 min.

Roissybus leaves every 15 min. for Paris Opéra.

Orly Rail (RER line C) takes 35 minutes from Orly airport to the centre of Paris.

Air France buses from Orly take 30 minutes.

Orlyval automatic métro runs every 4 to 8 minutes during the day, for a journey of approximately 30 minutes.

A *taxi* to the centre of Paris will cost about 130F from Orly and 180F from Roissy–Charles-de-Gaulle.

Taxis. The running charge is displayed on a meter. It consists of an initial fixed fee (13F), plus the price of the journey, with a tariff varying according to the time of day. Pickups at train stations or at Air France terminals entail an extra charge of 18F; baggage, 6F for every piece over 5 kg; an animal, 4F. In principle, taxis are not obliged to carry more than three passengers. The driver may be persuaded to consent to a fourth, but he will charge a supplement of 10F.

Complaints are handled by the Service des Taxis, Préfecture de Police, 36, rue des Morillons, 75015 Paris, tel. 01 55 76 20 16. Be prepared to give the taxi number, date, time and reason for complaint.

SNCF Trains. For information or reservations, call (7 a.m.–10 p.m.): Ile-de-France, tel. 01 45 65 60 00; national lines, tel. 01 45 82 50 50.

INDEX

General editor:	Barbara Ender-Jones
Text:	Ken Bernstein, Barbara Ender-Jones
The Hard Facts:	Alice Taucher
Additional research:	Philippe Bénet
Layout:	André Misteli
Photos:	covers, pp. 8, 28, 45, 50 Hémisphères;
	pp. 4, 7, 14, 21, 37 Claude Huber
	Maps: Elsner & Schichor

Printed in Switzerland. 9/705–25

The French Way

Bonjour!
Hello!

Bonjour!   Hello!

You can't just walk into a shop or office or café in France without greeting whoever is there; it would be rude. Offer a *"bonjour"* to the waiter, the barman, the baker… and get one back, with a smile. (After about 5 p.m., switch to *"bonsoir".)*

Always tack on to such a phrase *"Madame"*, *"Monsieur"* or *"Mademoiselle"*. Being courteous in France has nothing to do with social rank as the use of "madam" or "sir" might imply in English.

Shaking hands is common. But the French don't try to show how strong or sincere they are with the strength of the grip. A firm but looser and briefer shake is in order.

Greeting friends, kissing on the cheeks is the norm between men and women or between women, and increasingly between men. Both cheeks are involved, usually starting with the right cheek. A near-miss will do. An accompanying puckering grunt is not necessary. Gentlemen rarely kiss ladies' hands any more. It's a lost art.

Polite people in all countries are generous in the use of "please" *(s'il vous plaît)* and "thank you" *(merci)*. The French never skimp on these courteous formulas. Don't hesitate to follow suit.

Striking up a conversation is easy. But personal questions like "What do you do?", not to mention "How much do you earn?", are out of bounds.

Don't be shy. To help you with your spoken French we provide a very simple transcription. You may not sound like a native Parisian, but people will be pleased that you're trying. French has a few sounds unknown in English. For instance the underlined <u>*n*</u> indicates that the preceding vowel is a nasal sound. Another tricky sound we write *ew*. Purse your lips for "oo" while pronouncing "ee".

Hello.	Bonjour, madame/ monsieur.	bohn-zhoor, mah-dahm/ muh-syuh
Good morning/after-noon.	Bonjour.	bohn-zhoor
Good evening.	Bonsoir.	bohn-swahr
Good night.	Bonne nuit.	bon nwee
Goodbye.	Au revoir.	oh ruh-vwahr
See you later.	A bientôt.	ah byan-toh
Hi!/Bye!	Salut!	sah-lew
Yes.	Oui.	wee
No.	Non.	nohn
Maybe.	Peut-être.	puh-tehtr
That's fine/Okay.	D'accord.	dah-kohr
That's right!	Tout à fait!	too tah feh
Please.	S'il vous plaît.	seel voo pleh
Thank you/Thanks.	Merci.	mehr-see
Thank you very much.	Merci beaucoup.	mehr-see boh-koo
You're welcome.	De rien.	duh ryan
Nice to meet you.	Enchanté.	ahn-shahn-teh
How are you?	Comment allez-vous?	koh-mahn tah-leh-voo
Well, thanks. And you?	Bien, merci. Et vous?	byan, mehr-see. eh voo
Pardon me.	Pardon.	pahr-dohn
I'm (very) sorry.	Désolé.	deh-zoh-leh
Don't mention it.	Il n'y a pas de quoi.	eel nyah pah duh kwah
Excuse me.	Excusez-moi.	ehks-kew-zeh-mwah
My name is...	Je m'appelle...	zhuh mah-pehl
I don't understand.	Je ne comprends pas.	zhuh nuh kohn-prahn pah
Slowly, please.	Pas trop vite!	pah troh veet
Could you say that again, please?	Pouvez-vous répéter, s'il vous plaît?	poo-veh-voo reh-peh-teh, seel voo pleh
Do you speak English?	Parlez-vous anglais?	pahr-leh-voo ahn-gleh
Let's go.	Allons-y.	ah-lohn-zee

Taxi! Taxi!

Since taxi drivers everywhere tend to be talkative, this may be your chance to practise your French—if you can get a word in edgeways! If you don't see a taxi prowling for business, you'll soon find a stand where they wait for customers. The taxi meter measures the basic fare but there may be extras, such as stowing baggage in the trunk. When at last the grand total is revealed, a 10 percent tip is welcomed.

Métro. In Paris, the *métro* (subway) is the fastest, most efficient way to travel. For longer trips in the city and out to the suburbs the complementary RER system is even faster. To change lines, follow the sign *Correspondance*. Exit is *Sortie*.

Tickets are sold singly or in batches of ten *("un carnet")* from machines and booths inside the *métro* stations and, aboveground, at newsstands and *tabacs* (stores and cafés licensed to sell tobacco).

Your *métro* tickets are also valid on any Paris bus. This is a more leisurely but comfortable way—outside rush-hour—to get around while seeing some scenery.

Inter-city. The French National Railways, SNCF, serve thousands of destinations all over the country. For the world's fastest train, the TGV *(train à grande vitesse),* you need advance reservations. After you've bought your ticket, you must validate it *(composter)* before entering the platform by punching it in an orange-coloured machine.

There are inter-city buses, as well, for inexpensive long-distance travel. Details at any bus terminal *(gare routière).*

---

24 Hours a Day. Trains are only one of the many aspects of French life that use the 24-hour clock. Remember 1 p.m. is 13.00 or *treize heures* and take it from there. If this is a problem, stick to morning trains!

Taxi, please!	**Taxi!**	tahk-see
Are you free?	**Etes-vous libre?**	eht-voo leebr
Hotel Palace, please.	**A l'Hôtel Palace, s'il vous plaît.**	ah loh-tehl pah-lahss, seel voo pleh
To the airport / the station, please.	**A l'aéroport/la gare, s'il vous plaît.**	ah lah-eh-roh-pohr / lah gahr, seel voo pleh
I'm in a hurry.	**Je suis pressé.**	zhuh swee preh-seh
Please stop here.	**Arrêtez ici, s'il vous plaît.**	ah-reh-teh zee-see, seel voo pleh
Please wait for me.	**Attendez-moi un moment.**	ah-tahn-deh-mwah uhn moh-mahn
How much is it?	**C'est combien?**	seh kohn-byan
Keep the change.	**Gardez la monnaie.**	gahr-deh lah moh-neh
Where is the métro, please?	**Où est le métro, s'il vous plaît?**	oo eh luh meh-troh, seel voo pleh
A book of tickets, please.	**Un carnet, s'il vous plaît.**	uhn kahr-neh, seel voo pleh
one-way	**aller simple**	ah-leh sanpl
round-trip	**aller-retour**	ah-leh ruh-toor
first class	**première classe**	pruh-myehr klahss
second class	**seconde classe**	suh-gohnd klahss
platform	**quai**	keh
toilets	**toilettes**	twah-leht
stop	**arrêt**	ah-reh
Is this seat free?	**Cette place est-elle libre?**	seht plahss eh-tehl leebr

You and You. There are two kinds of "you" in French. *Vous* is formal and also plural. *Tu* is for addressing children, close friends and family, and animals. Young people use *tu* among themselves, even to strangers. When in doubt, play it safe with *vous*. The dog won't bite, though his owner might smile.

Concierge Hall porter

People working at the desk of your hotel are almost bound to know a foreign language—or several. But it's always agreeable to offer a phrase or two in French. When dealing with the chambermaid you'll probably have to rely on French, perhaps accompanied by sign language for the subtleties.

Incidentally, tipping is part of the culture, so don't forget the bellboy who carries your bags, the maid if you're staying more than a few days, and the concierge if he or she solves a problem for you. Thanks to years of training and a network of local contacts, concierges take pride in doing the almost-impossible: unearthing a couple of last-minute tickets to the opera or a table at one of the best restaurants.

The tourism authorities rate French hotels in five categories according to the comforts offered, from one star to four stars and an L for Luxury class at the very top of the line. An *hôtel garni* has no restaurant, but breakfast is part of the deal. At the other end of the scale, you can stay in a *château-hôtel*. But don't move your luggage into that splendid building labelled *Hôtel de Ville*. That's the town hall.

False Friends. Many French words look like direct equivalents of English words, but you could be very wrong. A few examples of what the French call *faux amis* (false friends), and what they *really* mean:

car	bus, coach
circulation	traffic
demander	ask a question
forfait	package deal
librairie	bookshop
monnaie	coins, change
pile	battery (camera, pocket torch)
slip	underpants

Here's the confirmation/ voucher.	Voici la confirmation/ le bon.	vwah-see lah kohn-feer-mah-syohn/luh bohn
a single room	une chambre simple	ewn shahnbr sanpl
a double	une chambre double	ewn shahnbr doobl
twin beds	lits jumeaux	lee zhew-moh
double bed	grand lit	grahn lee
with a bath/shower	avec bain/douche	ah-vehk ban/doosh
My key, please.	Ma clef, s'il vous plaît.	mah kleh, seel voo pleh
Is there mail for me?	Y a-t-il du courrier pour moi?	yah-teel dew koo-ryeh poor mwah
I need:	Il me faut:	eel muh foh
hangers	des cintres	deh santr
soap	du savon	dew sah-vohn
a blanket	une couverture	ewn koo-vehr-tewr
a different pillow	un autre oreiller	uhn nohtr oh-reh-yeh
These are clothes to be washed.	Voici du linge à laver.	vwah-see dew lanzh ah lah-veh
These are clothes to be cleaned/ pressed.	Voici des vêtements à nettoyer/ à repasser.	vwah-see deh veht-mahn ah neh-twah-yeh/ ah ruh-pah-seh
Urgently.	C'est urgent.	seh tewr-zahn
I'm checking out.	Je quitte l'hôtel.	zhuh keet loh-tehl
I'd like to pay by credit card.	Je voudrais payer avec ma carte de crédit.	zhuh voo-dreh peh-yeh ah-vehk mah kahrt duh kreh-dee

A Hint About Pronunciation. In a French word, the final "e" and most final consonants are silent. However, if the next word begins with a vowel, the final consonant is often pronounced and the two words run together. We have shown this liaison as if the second word began with a consonant. Usually, "ll" is pronounced like the "y" in "year", and "qu" like "k".

La carte, s'il vous plaît! Menu, please!

In France, eating is an art, so culture-lovers don't mind spending a couple of hours over lunch. To help you choose a restaurant, the law requires that the menu and prices be displayed outside. In addition to a multitude of choices you could make from the à la carte menu there is normally a fixed-price menu or *menu du jour*. This may offer choices for each of three courses. The set menus tend to be substantially less expensive than the sum of their ingredients.

If time is money, you'll find no shortage of fast-food establishments, takeaway stands, and self-service restaurants.

Breakfast *(petit déjeuner)* can be any time. Cafés serve coffee and croissants or rolls all morning. Lunch *(déjeuner)*, the main event for many French, starts around 12.30 or 1 p.m.

Dinner *(dîner)*, the evening meal, gets going at 8 or 8.30 p.m. Some places stop serving around 10 to 10.30 p.m.

French waiters are reputed to be haughty and difficult, but most of the time they are merely maintaining their professional distance from the client. Yet they can be extremely helpful in describing mysteriously named items and recommending alternatives. Just don't expect first-name chumminess or, at the other extreme, any hint of subservience.

Wine is so complex a subject that it fills whole bookshelves as well as cellars. Generally it comes in three colours —red *(rouge)*, white *(blanc)* and pink *(rosé)*. Don't hesitate to ask for detailed advice from your waiter or the specialist wine waiter *(sommelier)*. For the undemanding, an open wine, usually quite respectable and reasonably priced, is served *en carafe*. Beer is okay, too.

Tipping Tip. Fifteen percent service charge *(service compris)* is usually included in the bill. If you've been competently served, leave some loose change as well for an extra tip.

I'm hungry/thirsty.	J'ai faim/soif.	zheh fan/swahf
A table for two, please.	Une table pour deux, s'il vous plaît.	ewn tahbl poor duh, seel voo pleh
The menu, please.	La carte, s'il vous plaît.	lah kahrt, seel voo pleh
The fixed menu, please.	Le menu, s'il vous plaît.	luh muh-new, seel voo pleh
I'm a vegetarian.	Je suis végétarien.	zhuh swee veh-zheh-tah-ryan
The wine list, please.	La carte des vins, s'il vous plaît.	lah kahrt deh van, seel voo pleh
A glass of red/white/rosé wine.	Un verre de vin rouge/blanc/rosé.	uhn vehr duh van roozh/blahn/roh-zeh
beef	bœuf	buhf
bread	pain	pan
butter	beurre	buhr
cheese	fromage	froh-mahzh
chicken	poulet	poo-leh
coffee	café	kah-feh
fish	poisson	pwah-sohn
fruit juice	jus de fruits	zhew duh frwee
ice cream	glace	glahss
meat	viande	vyahnd
milk	lait	leh
mineral water (fizzy/flat)	eau minérale (gazeuse/plate)	oh mee-neh-rahl (gah-zuhz/plaht)
mustard	moutarde	moo-tahrd
pork	porc	pohr
salt and pepper	sel et poivre	sehl eh pwahvr
tea	thé	teh
vegetables	légumes	leh-gewm
The bill, please.	L'addition, s'il vous plaît.	lah-dee-syohn, seel voo pleh

Ne quittez pas!   Hold on, please.

The French telephone system, drastically overhauled in recent years, is now the envy of much of the world. From public telephones on the street, showing instructions in several languages, you can phone any other country. Dial 00 for international, and the country code you're calling, followed by the area code and the local number. It really is very simple. Buy a *Télécarte,* a phonecard, sold at post offices, newsstands, *tabacs* and other outlets. Phoning home from your hotel room can be expensive unless you use an international phone card.

Post offices, identified by the yellow sign saying *La Poste,* provide a myriad of services from parcels to faxes and photocopies over a long working day—usually from 8 a.m. to 7 p.m. weekdays and until noon on Saturdays. If you want pretty stamps for your postcards, go to the window marked *Timbres de collection;* at the normal stamp counter they're liable to label your mail colourlessly from the postage meter machine. Beyond the post office, stamps are sold at the *bureau de tabac.* Letter boxes are yellow and bear the post office's logo, a stylized bird in flight.

Number, Please. French telephone numbers are longer than most; they are spoken in pairs, so 01 12 34 56 78 is *zero un douze trente-quatre cinquante-six soixante-dix-huit*—a mouthful by any standard.
  But to start at the beginning:

1 un	5 cinq	9 neuf	13 treize	17 dix-sept
2 deux	6 six	10 dix	14 quatorze	18 dix-huit
3 trois	7 sept	11 onze	15 quinze	19 dix-neuf
4 quatre	8 huit	12 douze	16 seize	20 vingt

May I use this phone?	Puis-je utiliser ce téléphone?	pweezh ew-tee-lee-zeh suh teh-leh-fohn
Can I reverse the charges?	Puis-je téléphoner en PCV?	pweezh teh-leh-foh-neh ahn peh-seh-veh
Wrong number.	Faux numéro.	foh new-meh-roh
Speak more slowly, please.	Plus lentement, s'il vous plaît.	plew lahnt-mahn, seel voo pleh
Could you take a message?	Puis-je laisser un message?	pweezh leh-seh uhn meh-sahzh
My number is…	Mon numéro est le…	mohn new-meh-roh eh luh
My room number is…	Mon numéro de chambre est le…	mohn new-meh-roh duh shahnbr eh luh
Do you sell stamps?	Vendez-vous des timbres?	vahn-deh voo deh tanbr
How much is it to Great Britain?	Combien est-ce pour la Grande-Bretagne?	kohn-byan ehss poor lah grahnd bruh-tahn-yuh
I'd like to mail this parcel.	Je voudrais expédier ce colis.	zhuh voo-dreh ehks-peh-dyeh suh koh-lee
Can I send a fax?	Puis-je envoyer un fax?	pweezh ahn-vwah-yeh uhn fahks
Can I make a photo-copy here?	Puis-je faire une photocopie ici?	pweezh fehr ewn foh-toh-koh-pee eesee
Where's the letter box?	Où est la boîte aux lettres?	oo eh lah bwaht oh lehtr
registered letter	lettre recommandée	lehtr ruh-koh-mahn-deh
air mail	par avion	pahr ah-vyohn
postcard	carte postale	kahrt poh-stahl

Happy Talk. Build up your vocabulary with a few useful, cheery adjectives: *sympathique* (charming), *splendide* (magnificent), *fantastique* (terrific), *formidable* (tremendous).

Combien?   How much?

The franc is the unit of currency, divided into 100 centimes. Prices may be written like this: 10F50, 10,50 F or 10.50 F (10 francs and 50 centimes). Banknotes start at 20 F, and coins range from 5 centimes to 20 F.

Hotels usually change foreign currency or traveller's cheques into French francs but the exchange rate is less generous than at a bank. Currency exchange offices *(bureaux de change)* also offer longer hours but usually smaller returns. In these speculative days, they are highly competitive, so it may be worth shopping around for the best rates.

Most banks are open from 9 a.m. to 4.30 p.m., Monday to Friday. Always take along your passport when changing money. (You can also make use of cashpoint machines linked up with your bank or credit card.)

Credit cards of the big international firms are widely accepted in hotels, restaurants and stores.

Shopping, from high-fashion boutique to antique flea market, is one of the pleasures of France. The big department stores are geared to foreign customers, with interpreters, currency exchange offices and shipping services. Elegant boutiques are found in all the fashionable neighbourhoods. Stores usually open around 9.30 a.m. and close between 6.30 and 7 p.m., Monday to Saturday. Except for the department stores, some may close for lunch hour.

Question Mark. There are any number of ways of formulating a question in French, some quite complicated. But a simple alternative can save you all the problems. Just make a statement but raise your voice to a higher note at the end of the sentence. *Voilà!* It's a question.

It's far away.	**C'est loin.**
Is it far away?	**C'est loin?**

currency exchange	change	shah<u>n</u>zh
Where can I change money?	Où puis-je changer de l'argent?	oo pweezh shah<u>n</u>-zheh duh lahr-zhah<u>n</u>
Can you cash a traveller's cheque?	Pouvez-vous encaisser un traveller?	poo-veh-voo ah<u>n</u>-keh-seh uh<u>n</u> trav-luhr
I want to change dollars/pounds sterling	Je veux changer des dollars/livres sterling	zhuh vuh shah<u>n</u>-zheh deh doh-lahr/lee-vruh stehr-leeng
Will this credit card do?	Acceptez-vous cette carte de crédit?	ahk-sehp-teh-voo seht kahrt duh kreh-dee
Can you help me?	Pouvez-vous m'aider?	poo-veh-voo meh-deh
Just looking...	Je voudrais juste regarder...	zhuh voo-dreh zhewst ruh-gahr-deh
How much is this?	C'est combien?	seh koh<u>n</u>-bya<u>n</u>
cheap	bon marché	boh<u>n</u> mahr-sheh
expensive	cher	shehr
Can I try it on?	Puis-je l'essayer?	pweezh leh-seh-yeh
I don't know the European sizes.	Je ne connais pas les tailles européennes.	zhuh nuh koh-neh pah leh tigh uh-roh-peh-ehn
I'll think about it.	Je vais réfléchir.	zhuh veh reh-fleh-sheer
I'll buy it.	Je le prends.	zhuh luh prah<u>n</u>
It's a gift.	C'est pour offrir.	seh poor oh-freer
A receipt, please.	Une facture, s'il vous plaît.	ewn fahk-tewr, seel voo pleh
antique shop	antiquaire	ah<u>n</u>-tee-kehr
bakery	boulangerie	boo-lah<u>n</u>zh-ree
delicatessen	traiteur	treh-tuhr
flea market	marché aux puces	mahr-sheh oh pewss
jewellery store	bijouterie	bee-zhoo-tree
pastry shop	pâtisserie	pah-tee-sree
second-hand shop	brocante	broh-kah<u>n</u>t
supermarket	supermarché	sew-pehr-mahr-sheh

Au secours!   Help!

High living is the culprit in most cases of tourists in distress —visitors overdoing the food and wine and nightlife for which France is famous. For solving small health problems look for the green cross identifying a chemists—*pharmacie*. Normally one pharmacy in every town (or district in big cities) stays open nights and weekends. If the worst should happen, Paris has two English-speaking hospitals. At least you won't have to memorize a big anatomical vocabulary. For an ambulance, anywhere in France, dial **18**.

Playing Safe. Cities everywhere have their share of crime. It's only prudent not to tempt fate—and pick-pockets—by carrying vulnerable handbags and wallets. Showy jewellery should also be avoided. And don't go out with any more cash than you're really going to need.

Lawmen. Although they're not reputed to be as friend-ly as the British bobbies, French police do try to be helpful to visitors. You're most likely to deal with the blue-uni-formed *police municipale,* who direct traffic and investigate crimes. (Remember to start any conversation with *"Bonjour, Monsieur".*) Their head-quarters is the *Commissariat,* not the *Gendarmerie.* In Paris, they are known as *agents de police.* To call the police anywhere in France, dial **17**.

Notices. The meaning of some signs you'll see:

Dames (or Femmes)	Ladies
Défense de fumer	No smoking
Entrée	Entrance
Fermé	Closed
Hors service	Out of order
Interdit	Forbidden
Messieurs (or Hommes)	Gentlemen
Sortie	Exit

I don't feel well.	Je ne me sens pas bien.	zhuh nuh muh sahn pah byan
Where is there a pharmacy?	Où se trouve une pharmacie?	oo suh troov ewn fahr-mah-see
an upset stomach	une indigestion	ewn an-dee-zheh-styohn
an injury	une blessure	ewn bleh-sewr
toothache	mal aux dents	mahl oh dahn
headache	migraine	mee-grehn
I have a pain...	J'ai mal...	zheh mahl
... in my leg	... à la jambe	ah lah zhahnb
... in my stomach	... au ventre	oh vahntr
... in my chest	... à la poitrine	ah lah pwah-treen
I am bleeding.	Je saigne.	zhuh seh-nyuh
I need a doctor.	J'ai besoin d'un médecin.	zheh buh-swan duhn mehd-san
I feel dizzy.	J'ai des vertiges.	zheh deh vehr-teezh
Can you give me a prescription?	Pouvez-vous me donner une ordonnance?	poo-veh-voo muh doh-neh ewn ohr-doh-nahnss
Help!	Au secours!	oh skoor
Stop thief!	Au voleur!	oh voh-lewr
Leave me alone.	Laissez-moi tranquille.	leh-seh mwah trahn-kee
I've lost my wallet/ passport.	J'ai perdu mon portefeuille/ mon passeport.	zheh pehr-dew mohn pohrt-fuhy/ mohn pah-spohr
My credit cards have been stolen.	On m'a volé mes cartes de crédit.	ohn mah voh-leh meh kahrt duh kreh-dee
I'm lost.	Je suis perdu.	zhuh swee pehr-dew
Where's the police station/the hospital?	Où se trouve le commissariat/l'hôpital?	oo suh troov luh koh-mee-sahr-yah/loh-pee-tahl
I have been assaulted.	J'ai été agressé.	zheh eh-teh ah-greh-seh
witness/lawyer	témoin/avocat	teh-mwan/ah-voh-kah

THE FRENCH WAY: INDEX

Signs Around Town:

Ascenseur	Lift/elevator
Caisse	Cashier
Complet	Full/no vacancies
Fermé	Closed
Piétons	Pedestrians
Poussez	Push
Soldes	Sale
Sonnez, s.v.p.	Please ring the bell
Sortie de secours	Emergency exit
Tirez	Pull

Useful Addresses and Phone Numbers in Paris

American consulate: 2, rue St-Florentin, 1st arr., tel. 01 43 12 22 22
Australian consulate: 4 rue Jean-Rey, 15th arr., tel. 01 40 59 33 00
British consulate: 35 rue du Faubourg Saint-Honoré, 8th arr.,
   tel. 01 44 51 31 00
Canadian consulate: 35 av. Montaigne, 8th arr., tel. 01 44 43 29 00
Irish consulate: 12 av. Foch, 16th arr., tel. 01 44 17 67 00
New Zealand consulate: 7ter rue Léonard-de-Vinci, 16th arr.,
   tel. 01 45 00 24 11
South African consulate: 59 Quai d'Orsay, 17th arr.,
   tel. 01 53 59 23 23
Paris Visitors & Convention Bureau English language informa-
   tion: tel. 01 49 52 53 54

JPM Publications SA • *Specialists in customized guides*

12, avenue William-Fraisse, 1006 Lausanne, Switzerland
Copyright © 1997, 1996 JPM Publications SA – Printed in Switzerland